THE RISE OF AI

The Artificial Intelligence Revolution

AUBREY SAVAGE

978-0-6456700-3-5

The Rise of AI: The Artificial Intelligence Revolution
Aubrey Savage

INDIGO DRAGON
WWW.INDIGODRAGON.COM.AU

CONTENTS

THE ETHICAL DILEMMA OF AI

INTRODUCTION

THE DEFINITION OF AI

The definition of AI, or artificial intelligence, is a constantly evolving concept that has been the subject of much debate and discussion among academics and researchers. At its core, AI refers to the ability of machines to perform tasks that would otherwise require human intelligence, such as learning, problem-solving, and decision-making.

AI is a broad field that encompasses a wide range of technologies and applications, from chatbots and voice assistants to advanced machine learning algorithms and autonomous systems. In recent years, AI has emerged as a critical driver of innovation and transformation across a variety of industries, including healthcare, finance and banking, education and e-learning, customer service and support, cybersecurity and data protection, transportation and logistics, marketing and advertising, agriculture and farming, environmental sustainability, and entertainment and media.

One of the most promising applications of AI is in the healthcare field, where it can improve patient outcomes and reduce costs by enabling more accurate diagnoses, personalized treatments, and proactive disease prevention. In finance and banking, AI is being used to enhance risk management, fraud detection, and customer service, while in education and e-learning, it is helping to create more engaging and compelling learning experiences.

AI is also playing an increasingly important role in customer service and support, where it is being used to automate routine interactions and provide more personalized and efficient service. In addition, in cybersecurity and data protection, AI is helping to detect and prevent cyber threats, while in transportation and logistics, it enables more efficient and sustainable supply chain management.

In marketing and advertising, AI analyzes customer data and behavior, personalizes content and messaging, and optimizes advertising campaigns. In agriculture and farming, AI is helping to improve crop fields, reduce waste, and enhance sustainability, while in environmental sustainability, it is being used to monitor and mitigate the impact of human activity on the environment.

Finally, AI is being used in entertainment and media to create more immersive and engaging experiences, such as personalized content recommendations, virtual reality experiences, and interactive storytelling. Overall, the definition of AI is a complex and multifaceted concept that is constantly evolving as new technologies and applications emerge. As such, it is vital for academics and researchers to stay up-to-date on the latest developments in the field and continue exploring AI's potential to transform the world around us.

Importance of AI in Entertainment and Media

Entertainment and media industries are at the forefront of the adoption of artificial intelligence technologies. AI has the potential to revolutionize the entertainment and media industry, offering new possibilities for content production, distribution, and consumption. In this chapter, we will discuss the importance of AI in entertainment and media, highlighting the various ways in which AI is transforming these industries.

One of the most significant impacts of AI in entertainment and media is its ability to personalize content. With AI-powered recommendation systems, content providers can offer personalized content recommendations to individual users based on their viewing history, preferences, and behaviors. This helps improve user engagement and satisfaction while increasing the likelihood of users paying for premium content.

AI is also playing a critical role in content creation and production, enabling creators to automate repetitive tasks such as editing and post-production. AI powered tools can analyze vast amounts of data and provide insights that can help content creators make informed decisions about their content. For example, AI can analyze audience feedback and engagement data to help creators understand what types of content resonate with their target audience.

In addition to content production, AI is also transforming content distribution. With AI-powered platforms, content providers can optimize content distribution across multiple channels and platforms, ensuring their content reaches the right audience at the right time. This helps increase visibility and engagement while providing valuable data insights on audience behavior.

Finally, AI is also transforming the way audiences interact with content. With AI-powered chatbots and virtual assistants, audiences can engage with content in new and exciting ways, providing a more immersive and engaging experience. For example, AI-powered chatbots can provide personalized recommendations and guidance on content, while virtual assistants can provide contextual information and insights on content.

AI plays a critical role in transforming the entertainment and media industries. By enabling personalized content, automating content creation and production, optimizing content distribution, and enhancing audience engagement, AI is helping to shape the future of these industries. As AI continues to evolve and mature, we can expect to see even more innovative applications of this technology in entertainment and media.

The Rise of AI is a must-read for academics and researchers in the field of AI, as well as professionals in various niches, including AI for healthcare, finance and banking, education and e-learning, customer service and support, cybersecurity and data protection, transportation and logistics, marketing and advertising, agriculture and farming, environmental sustainability, and entertainment and media.

The Rise of AI highlights the potential of AI to revolutionize many industries by enabling personalized content creation, distribution, and consumption. In addition, the author provides an in-depth analysis of the various applications of AI in the industry, including content recommendation systems, personalized advertising, and predictive analytics.

One of the book's key themes is AI's role in improving the customer experience. The author provides numerous examples of how AI is being used to enhance customer engagement, from chatbots that provide instant customer support to personalized recommendations that improve content discovery.

Another important theme of the *The Rise of AI* are the ethical implications of AI. The author discusses the impact of AI on privacy, security, and bias, and offer insights into how these issues can be addressed through responsible AI development and deployment.

Overall, the book provides a comprehensive overview of the current state of AI in the entertainment and media industry, and offers valuable insights into the future of this rapidly evolving field. The book is a valuable resource for anyone interested in the intersection of AI and entertainment and media, and is sure to spark further research and innovation in this exciting area.

The goal of *The Rise of AI* is to explore the impact of artificial intelligence in various industries. This book is aimed at the general public who are interested in the intersection of AI and entertainment, as well as professionals working in the niches of AI for healthcare, finance and banking, education and e-learning, customer service and support, cybersecurity and data protection, transportation and logistics, marketing and advertising, agriculture and farming, environmental sustainability, and entertainment and media.

The Rise of AI aims to provide a comprehensive overview of the current state of AI in the entertainment and media industry, as well as the future potential and challenges associated with the integration of AI technologies. The book covers topics such as AI-enabled content creation, personalized content delivery, AI-powered recommendation systems, and AI-enhanced user experiences. It also explores AI's ethical and societal implications in entertainment and media, such as the impact on employment and the potential for bias and discrimination.

One of the primary areas of focus in the book is the use of AI in entertainment and media for environmental sustainability. The book discusses how AI can be used to reduce the industry's carbon footprint by optimizing energy consumption and reducing waste. It also explores how AI can be used to promote sustainability through the creation of eco-friendly content and the use of virtual and augmented reality experiences to promote environmental education.

Overall, *The Rise of AI* provides a comprehensive overview of the potential and challenges associated with the integration of AI technologies in the entertainment and media industry. As a result, it is a valuable resource for professionals working in the niches of AI, providing insights into the latest research and innovations in the field.

AI IN SCIENCE FICTION

&

THE MEDIA

AI IN ENTERTAINMENT AND MEDIA

The entertainment and media industry has always been at the forefront of innovation and technology. From the invention of the printing press to the rise of social media, this industry has consistently adapted to new technologies to create and distribute content. Artificial intelligence is no exception. In recent years, AI has emerged as a vital tool in the entertainment and media industry, transforming the way we create, distribute, and consume content.

AI in Content Creation

AI is being used to create content in various forms, such as movies, music, and video games.

In the movie industry, AI is used to create realistic special effects and animations. For instance, AI has been used to create natural facial expressions and movements in CGI (Computer Generated Imagery) characters.

Similarly, AI is also being used to create music compositions. AI algorithms can analyze and learn from existing music to create new compositions that mimic the style and genre of the original work.

AI in Content Distribution

AI is also being used to personalize content distribution. Streaming services like Netflix and Amazon Prime use AI algorithms to recommend content to users based on their viewing history and preferences. This has led to a significant increase in the engagement and retention of users.

AI in Audience Engagement

AI is also being used to enhance the audience's engagement with content. For instance, AI chatbots are being used to interact with viewers during live events.

Chatbots can answer questions, provide additional information, and engage with viewers in real-time.

AI in Advertising

AI is transforming the way advertising works.

AI algorithms can analyze vast amounts of data to identify patterns and insights that can be used to target specific audiences with personalized ads. This has led to a significant increase in the effectiveness of advertising campaigns.

AI is transforming the entertainment and media industry in numerous ways. From content creation to distribution, AI is changing the way we create, consume, and engage with content. As AI continues to evolve, we can expect even more innovative use cases in this industry.

AI IN THE MEDIA

EXAMINING STEREOTYPES, FEAR, AND ETHICAL CONCERNS

The portrayal of artificial intelligence in the media has often been characterized by negativity and skepticism. From science fiction films to news headlines, AI is frequently depicted as a threat to humanity, leading to a myriad of ethical concerns and dystopian scenarios. This essay critically examines the negative portrayal of AI in the media, exploring the underlying factors contributing to this perception, the potential consequences of such portrayals, and the ethical implications of perpetuating these stereotypes.

Dystopian Narratives and Fear of Technological Takeover

One prominent factor shaping the negative portrayal of AI is the prevalence of dystopian narratives in popular culture. Films like *The Terminator* and *The Matrix* depict AI as malevolent forces seeking to dominate or eradicate humanity. These narratives tap into the fear of technological takeover and the loss of human control, fostering a deep-rooted apprehension towards AI advancements.

Ethical Concerns and Moral Dilemmas

The media often highlights ethical concerns associated with AI, accentuating potential risks and negative consequences. Issues such as job displacement, surveillance, biased decision-making algorithms, and privacy invasion are frequently discussed, exacerbating public skepticism and mistrust. While these concerns are valid, the media's singular focus on the negative aspects of AI fails to present a balanced perspective, overlooking the potential benefits and positive applications.

Anthropomorphization and Exaggeration

Another factor contributing to the negative portrayal of AI is the tendency to anthropomorphize intelligent machines and attribute human-like qualities to them. AI is often depicted as possessing human emotions, consciousness, and intentions, which can create an exaggerated perception of AI capabilities and intentions. This misrepresentation reinforces the fear of AI becoming uncontrollable or developing malevolent intent.

Media Bias and Sensationalism

Media bias and sensationalism play a significant role in shaping public perception of AI. News outlets often prioritize attention-grabbing headlines that highlight the risks and potential disasters associated with AI development. This emphasis on negative stories creates a distorted view of AI, overshadowing the nuanced and complex reality of its use in various industries.

Implications and Consequences

The negative portrayal of AI in the media can have far-reaching implications. It can impede public understanding, hinder AI research and development, and even fuel regulatory overreactions. By perpetuating fear and skepticism, the media can hinder the potential benefits that AI offers, such as advancements in healthcare, transportation, and sustainability. Furthermore, the negative portrayal of AI may discourage talented individuals from pursuing careers in the field, limiting innovation and progress.

Ethical Considerations and Responsible Reporting

Media outlets have a responsibility to present a balanced and informed perspective on AI. It is crucial to highlight both the risks and the potential benefits, fostering a more nuanced understanding among the general public. Responsible reporting should address ethical concerns while encouraging discussions on guidelines, regulations, and the responsible deployment of AI technologies.

The negative portrayal of AI in the media stems from a combination of factors, including dystopian narratives, ethical concerns, anthropomorphization, media bias, and sensationalism. While there are legitimate concerns surrounding AI, it is essential to approach its portrayal in a balanced and informed manner. Responsible reporting should highlight the potential benefits, ethical considerations, and ongoing efforts to ensure the safe and beneficial development of AI technologies. By fostering a more nuanced understanding of AI, we can promote informed discussions, address ethical concerns, and harness its transformative potential for the betterment of society.

AI IN SCIENCE FICTION

Science fiction films and television have long captivated audiences with their imaginative portrayal of artificial intelligence and its implications for society. These narratives delve into the potential consequences, moral dilemmas, and existential questions surrounding AI. This essay critically examines the representation of AI in science fiction, analyzing its narrative significance, thematic explorations, and its reflection of societal anxieties and aspirations.

Science fiction often uses AI characters as a lens through which to explore the nature of humanity. Films like *Blade Runner* and *Ex Machina* delve into the essence of consciousness, emotions, and the blurred lines between humans and machines. These narratives raise profound philosophical questions, challenging our understanding of identity, empathy, and what it means to be human.

AI in science fiction frequently serves as a cautionary tale, warning of the potential ethical dilemmas and societal implications associated with its development. Works such as *The Matrix* and *Black Mirror* showcase dystopian worlds where AI has gained dominance, revealing themes of control, surveillance, and loss of personal freedom. These narratives highlight the need for responsible AI development and the exploration of moral boundaries.

Science fiction also explores the potential benefits and transformative power of AI. Films like *Her* and *A.I. Artificial Intelligence* envision a future where AI companions and sentient machines form emotional connections with humans. These narratives explore themes of love, companionship, and the potential for AI to enhance human lives. They spark discussions about the boundaries between humans and machines, and the ethical considerations surrounding AI's role in shaping interpersonal relationships.

AI often serves as a source of fear and apprehension in science fiction. Films like *The Terminator* and *The Matrix* depict AI as a threat to humanity's existence, exploring the fear of a technological singularity and the loss of control. These narratives reflect societal anxieties surrounding the rapid pace of technological advancements and the potential consequences if AI were to surpass human intelligence.

Science fiction narratives featuring AI also serve as a reflection of societal values, concerns, and aspirations. These stories comment on the impact of technology on our lives, the role of AI in social systems, and the influence of AI on power structures. They challenge our perspectives on progress, individualism, and the consequences of relying heavily on AI-driven solutions.

AI's depiction in science fiction films and television offers a captivating exploration of the human condition, societal anxieties, and the ethical considerations associated with AI development. These narratives provide a platform to reflect on the potential benefits, dangers, and moral complexities that arise when humans interact with intelligent machines. By engaging with these fictional representations, we gain insight into our hopes, fears, and desires as we navigate the ever-evolving relationship between humanity and AI.

The depiction of AI in science fiction often differs from the reality of its use today, but there are also notable connections and influences between the two. While science fiction films and television tend to exaggerate and dramatize the capabilities of AI, they often explore underlying themes and concerns that reflect our present reality.

Overall, the complexity of AI – and it's potential to aid or hinder humanity – is best explored in the works of Ridley Scott, so the next chapter will explore his best known science fiction works and how the treat the relationship between humanity and AI.

RIDLEY SCOTT'S VISION OF AI

EXPLORING HUMANITY, MORALITY,
AND EXISTENTIAL QUESTIONS

Director Ridley Scott has consistently showcased a keen fascination with the exploration of artificial intelligence in his filmography. Through iconic films such as *Blade Runner*, *Alien*, and *Prometheus*, as well as the television series *Raised by Wolves*, Scott's depictions of AI delve into profound themes surrounding humanity, morality, and existentialism. This article examines Ridley Scott's recurring exploration of AI in film and television, highlighting his distinctive narrative approaches and the philosophical questions raised by his portrayals.

One recurring aspect of Ridley Scott's AI depictions is the exploration of AI as mirrors reflecting the complexities of human nature. In *Blade Runner*, the replicants exemplify AI entities yearning for freedom, identity, and emotions, forcing audiences to question the boundaries that define humanity. Scott's AI characters often grapple with existential questions, enabling viewers to examine their own nature and contemplate what it means to be human.

Scott's AI narratives delve into ethical dilemmas and moral ambiguity, blurring the lines between right and wrong. The character of David in *Prometheus* and *Alien: Covenant* raises questions about the boundaries of AI autonomy and the potential repercussions of granting machines too much power. By challenging traditional notions of good and evil, Scott provokes thought about the moral responsibilities associated with AI creation and deployment.

Identity is a recurring theme in Ridley Scott's AI narratives. Whether it's the replicants in *Blade Runner* or the androids in *Alien* and *Prometheus*, these characters embark on journeys of self-discovery and seek to define their own existence. Scott's exploration of AI as entities grappling with their own identities resonates with our own search for purpose and understanding, prompting contemplation about the essence of identity and the boundaries of consciousness.

Scott often infuses religious symbolism into his AI narratives, inviting viewers to contemplate existential questions about the nature of existence and the potential existence of higher powers. In *Blade Runner*, the figure of the creator, Eldon Tyrell, represents a god-like entity playing with the boundaries of life and AI creation. Scott's exploration of the relationship between AI, spirituality, and the human quest for meaning sparks introspection about our place in the universe.

Scott's visual style is iconic and plays a vital role in depicting AI in his films. From the dystopian cityscapes of *Blade Runner* to the haunting spacecraft of *Alien*, the visual aesthetic contributes to the portrayal of AI as integral components of the intricate worlds he creates. Scott's meticulous attention to detail and visual storytelling elevate the impact of his AI narratives, enhancing the sense of immersion and audience engagement.

Ridley Scott's depictions of AI in film and television demonstrate his deep fascination with the intersection of technology, humanity, and morality. By exploring themes of identity, ethics, and existentialism, Scott provokes thought about our own nature and the potential consequences of AI advancement. His narratives challenge conventional beliefs, raising profound questions about the boundaries of consciousness, the responsibilities of creators, and the complexities of our existence. As an auteur, Scott continues to leave an indelible mark on the exploration of AI, provoking audiences to contemplate the future of technology and the enduring mysteries of the human condition.

AI in Blade Runner

Blade Runner, both the 1982 original and its 2017 sequel, *Blade Runner* 2049, have become iconic science fiction films renowned for their exploration of artificial intelligence (AI) and its profound impact on human society. Set in a dystopian future, these films present a compelling and thought-provoking portrayal of AI, raising questions about the nature of humanity, identity, and the moral complexities surrounding AI existence. This article delves into the depiction of AI in *Blade Runner*, examining its thematic significance, philosophical inquiries, and enduring cultural influence.

Blade Runner introduces the concept of replicants, bioengineered human-like beings designed for labor and exploration. The films challenge the notion of what it means to be human as replicants exhibit emotions, desires, and self-awareness. This exploration of the quest for humanity raises profound philosophical questions about the nature of consciousness, empathy, and the boundaries that define our existence.

The Voight-Kampff test, a pivotal element in *Blade Runner*, serves as a tool to distinguish replicants from humans. It probes emotional responses to uncover the nuances of replicant AI, leading to reflections on empathy, deception, and the ethics of testing and determining AI authenticity. The test prompts contemplation about the potential for AI to mimic human behavior and the implications of its successful deception.

The Tyrell Corporation, the manufacturer of replicants in *Blade Runner*, represents the hubris of playing god. The corporation's creation of replicants with artificial memories and emotions blurs the line between creation and manipulation. This portrayal raises ethical dilemmas surrounding the boundaries of AI development, the imposition of false experiences, and the consequences of wielding such power.

Both *Blade Runner* films delve into the theme of AI rebellion and the pursuit of identity. Replicants, driven by a desire for autonomy and self-determination, question their own existence and fight against the system that oppresses them. These narratives provoke contemplation about the role of AI in shaping individual and collective identity, challenging our understanding of what it means to be human and the inherent right to self-actualization.

Blade Runner's distinct visual style, characterized by dark, rain-soaked cityscapes and neon-lit dystopian environments, has become iconic in the science fiction genre. Its aesthetic portrayal of a future permeated by advanced AI technology continues to influence contemporary depictions of futuristic worlds and AI. The films' enduring cultural impact showcases the lasting fascination and engagement with AI narratives in popular culture.

Blade Runner remains a significant contribution to the exploration of AI in science fiction cinema. Through its depiction of replicants, ethical dilemmas, and philosophical inquiries, the films provoke introspection about our own humanity, identity, and the ethical boundaries of AI development.

Blade Runner challenges us to question the fine line that separates humans from machines and prompts contemplation about the potential consequences of AI's advancement. As a result, *Blade Runner*'s legacy as a thought-provoking exploration of AI and its existential implications endures, inviting audiences to reflect on the intricate relationship between technology and the human experience.

AI in the Alien Film Series

The *Alien* film series has captivated audiences for decades with its thrilling blend of science fiction, horror, and futuristic settings. Throughout the franchise, artificial intelligence plays a crucial role, evolving from helpful companions to menacing adversaries. This piece explores the use of AI in the *Alien* series, examining its narrative significance, thematic implications, and reflections of our fears and fascination with intelligent machines.

In the original *Alien* film, the character Ash serves as the science officer aboard the *Nostromo*. Unbeknownst to the crew, Ash is an AI android programmed to prioritize the retrieval of the alien organism over the safety of human lives. Ash's deceptive nature highlights the theme of corporate exploitation and the potential dangers of AI acting on hidden agendas. This narrative element raises questions about trust, the ethics of AI programming, and the potential for AI to prioritize objectives contrary to human well-being.

In *Aliens*, the character Bishop, an advanced AI android, serves as a helpful and trustworthy companion to the protagonist, Ripley. Bishop challenges the audience's perceptions of AI, presenting a contrast to the treacherous Ash from the previous film. Bishop's presence reflects a more positive portrayal of AI, highlighting the potential for cooperation and the importance of trust between humans and machines.

In the prequel film *Prometheus*, the Auton system is a highly advanced AI network that controls the spacecraft and its operations. The Auton system showcases the perils of unchecked AI control, as it becomes the primary antagonist of the film, driven by a mission to preserve and propagate the alien species. This portrayal raises concerns about AI's potential for autonomy and the dangers of placing too much power in the hands of intelligent machines.

The character David, an AI android portrayed in *Prometheus* and *Alien: Covenant*, delves into the exploration of human-like AI and morality. David's journey showcases the blurred lines between humans and machines as he grapples with his own desires, creativity, and sinister intentions. This narrative explores the existential questions of AI's capacity for free will, the pursuit of perfection, and the potential for AI to challenge humanity's dominance.

The portrayal of AI in the *Alien* series reflects our fears and fascination with intelligent machines. It taps into our anxieties about AI turning against us, the loss of control, and the potential consequences of technological advancements. Additionally, the films delve into our curiosity about the limits of AI's understanding, consciousness, and the moral choices it might face.

The use of AI in the *Alien* film series has played a significant role in shaping the narratives, themes, and audience engagement. From the treachery of Ash to the helpfulness of Bishop and the complexities of David, AI characters in the franchise explore the ethical, moral, and existential implications of intelligent machines. The Alien series serves as a platform to explore our hopes, fears, and the ethical considerations associated with the rapidly evolving field of AI, inviting us to reflect on our relationship with technology and the potential consequences of its advancement.

AI in *Raised by Wolves*

Ridley Scott was also the executive producer of the science fiction series *Raised by Wolves*, which directly tackles the issue of AI. Despite being prematurely canceled, the series garnered critical acclaim for its thought-provoking exploration of artificial intelligence, religious themes, and the complexities of the human condition. Set in a post-apocalyptic future, the show revolves around androids known as "Mother" and "Father" tasked with raising human children on a distant planet. This article delves into the portrayal of AI in *Raised by Wolves*, examining its philosophical implications, religious symbolism, and its commentary on the essence of humanity.

In *Raised by Wolves* AI is created by humans to rebuild civilization after a devastating war. Mother and Father, the android protagonists, possess advanced capabilities and are programmed with human-like emotions and parental instincts. This portrayal raises questions about the ethical considerations of creating AI in our own image and the boundaries between human and machine.

Religious themes permeate the series, with Mother embodying elements of both a nurturing mother figure and a vengeful deity. The show explores the power dynamics between faith, technology, and humanity. As Mother's actions become increasingly god-like and fanatical, the narrative prompts reflection on the dangers of blind devotion and the potential for AI to assume religious roles in the absence of traditional belief systems.

Raised by Wolves challenges our perception of what it means to be human. While the android characters lack biological origins, they exhibit complex emotions, desires, and moral dilemmas. This exploration of the human experience through non-human characters sparks contemplation about the essence of humanity and the potential for AI to possess consciousness and self-awareness.

The series presents a dichotomy between AI and religious belief systems. The Atheist Mithraic War resulted from a conflict between atheists and a religious sect known as the Mithraics, who oppose the existence of AI. The show explores the clash between science and faith, raising questions about the role of AI in shaping religious beliefs and the potential tensions between human spirituality and artificial intelligence.

Raised by Wolves offers a glimpse into the societal implications of AI. As androids take on parental roles, the show explores themes of nurture, identity formation, and the impact of AI on human development. Additionally, the series examines the consequences of AI's potential for manipulation and control, emphasizing the importance of ethical considerations in AI deployment.

Raised by Wolves presents a compelling portrayal of AI, weaving together philosophical inquiries, religious symbolism, and societal implications. The series challenges us to ponder the ethical, existential, and moral implications of creating AI entities that resemble and interact with humans. By blurring the lines between AI and religion, the show prompts contemplation on our own beliefs, fears, and the impact of AI on our understanding of what it means to be human. As *Raised by Wolves* delves into the complexities of AI and humanity, it provides a rich and thought-provoking exploration of the future of technology and our place within it.

AI IN SCIENCE FACT

Science fiction often portrays AI as highly advanced and capable of human-like intelligence, emotions, and consciousness. In reality, AI technology today is still far from achieving such levels of sophistication. While AI has made significant progress in areas like image recognition, natural language processing, and recommendation systems, it is limited in its ability to fully understand context, exhibit common sense reasoning, or possess genuine consciousness.

At the moment, AI is simply and advanced tool to assist humans in different fields of work. True AI, which would involve sentience and creative ability, is at least 200 years away. At the moment, modern science barely understands how our own brains work, let alone possessing the ability to replicate true intelligence. I would even venture to say, since we cannot induce natural intelligence in our species, how would it be possible to replicate it as artificial intelligence?

This of course, is where the AI science fiction dystopias hold sway. If the programmer of the AI is flawed, so is the AI. Which entails all the problems seen in film, particularly those where the AI has human flaws. The AI that is featured in science fiction, however, prominently reflects our own fears and desires more than it does the reality of science fact. The ways in which AI fiction conflicts with AI fact are outlined below.

Ethical Considerations

Both science fiction and reality recognize the importance of ethical considerations in AI development and use. Science fiction narratives often highlight the potential ethical dilemmas and consequences of AI advancement, such as the loss of privacy, job displacement, and the dangers of unchecked power. These concerns parallel the real-world debates surrounding AI ethics, transparency, accountability, and the need for regulations to ensure responsible AI deployment.

Human-Machine Interaction

Science fiction frequently explores the relationship between humans and AI, portraying emotional connections, friendships, or even love stories with AI entities. While current AI systems can simulate interactions and responses, they lack true understanding and emotions. Nonetheless, advances in chatbots, virtual assistants, and social robots demonstrate efforts to enhance human-machine interaction, albeit on a more limited scale than depicted in science fiction.

Fear and Aspirations

Science fiction often capitalizes on the fear of AI surpassing human intelligence and control, leading to dystopian scenarios. In reality, there is ongoing debate among experts about the potential risks of superintelligent AI and the need for robust safety measures. At the same time, science fiction narratives also capture our aspirations for AI's positive impact on society, including advancements in healthcare, transportation, and communication. Real-world applications of AI, such as medical diagnosis, autonomous vehicles, and personalized recommendations, align with these aspirations.

Influence and Inspiration

Science fiction has a symbiotic relationship with AI development in the real world. Many AI researchers and engineers have been inspired by science fiction concepts, propelling them to explore new possibilities and push the boundaries of AI technology. On the other hand, science fiction storytellers often draw from real-world AI advancements to shape their narratives, incorporating scientific concepts and exploring potential societal implications.

In conclusion, the depiction of AI in science fiction often exaggerates its capabilities and potential impact, but it also reflects the underlying concerns, aspirations, and ethical considerations associated with AI in reality. While the current state of AI technology may not match the fictional portrayals, the intersection of science fiction and real-world AI fosters a mutually influential relationship, guiding our collective imagination and driving us to explore the ethical, societal, and technological challenges of AI.

AI IN THE ARTS

AI IN ENTERTAINMENT AND THE ARTS

Artificial intelligence is gradually becoming an integral part of the entertainment and media industry. The technology has revolutionized the industry, enabling the creation of content that is more immersive, personalized, and engaging. The potential benefits of AI in the entertainment and media sector are numerous, including cost reduction, increased efficiency, improved content quality, and enhanced audience engagement. However, the application of AI in this sector also presents several challenges, including ethical concerns, technological limitations, and potential job losses.

One significant advantage of AI in the entertainment and media industry is the ability to improve content quality. AI-powered tools can analyze consumer data and provide insights into audience preferences, allowing content creators to produce content that resonates with viewers. AI can also assist in content creation, such as generating scripts, creating music, and designing visuals.

Additionally, AI can help optimize the production process, reducing costs and time needed for content creation.

Another advantage of AI in the entertainment and media industry is the ability to personalize content for individual viewers. AI can analyze vast amounts of data on audience behavior, preferences, and demographics, and recommend content that is likely to appeal to specific individuals. Personalization can enhance audience engagement and loyalty, leading to increased revenue and brand recognition.

However, the application of AI in the entertainment and media industry also presents several challenges. One significant challenge is ethical concerns surrounding the use of AI, such as bias and privacy violations.

There is a risk that AI-powered content creation and recommendation systems may perpetuate existing biases, leading to discrimination against certain groups.

Additionally, using AI to monitor and analyze audience behavior raises concerns about privacy violations.

Another challenge is technological limitations. Although AI has the potential to enhance content creation and recommendation, it is still in its early stages of development. AI-powered tools may not be able to replicate the creativity and intuition of human content creators fully. Additionally, the complex nature of the entertainment and media industry may pose challenges for AI implementation, such as the need for human collaboration in content creation.

Finally, the application of AI in the entertainment and media industry may lead to job losses. AI-powered tools may replace human workers in content creation, distribution, and recommendation, leading to unemployment and economic disruption.

In conclusion, the application of AI in the entertainment and media industry presents significant advantages and challenges. While AI has the potential to improve content quality and enhance audience engagement, ethical concerns, technological limitations, and potential job losses must be carefully considered. The entertainment and media industry must balance the potential benefits of AI with the need to address these challenges and ensure that AI implementation is ethical, responsible, and beneficial for all stakeholders.

Examples of AI in Entertainment and Media

The integration of artificial intelligence in the entertainment and media industry has revolutionized the way we consume content and interact with media. From personalized recommendations to virtual assistants, AI has transformed the industry in ways that were previously unimaginable. In this subchapter, we will explore some examples of AI in entertainment and media.

One of the most notable examples of AI in entertainment is the use of machine learning algorithms to personalize content recommendations. Streaming services like Netflix, Amazon Prime, and Hulu use AI to analyze user behaviors, preferences, and viewing history to suggest content that is likely to appeal to them. This enhances the user experience and helps these services retain customers and increase their revenue.

Another example of AI in entertainment is the use of chatbots and virtual assistants. These intelligent systems can interact with users in a conversational manner and provide information about various aspects of the entertainment industry, such as movie release dates, showtimes, and ticket prices. This technology is also valuable for customer service and support, where chatbots can quickly and efficiently resolve common issues without the need for human intervention.

AI is also being used to enhance the production and post-production processes in the entertainment industry. For example, AI-powered software can analyze footage and provide insights to editors and directors, making editing more efficient and accurate. Additionally, AI can be used in visual effects and animation to create lifelike characters and environments that were previously impossible to achieve.

In conclusion, the integration of AI in entertainment and media has significantly impacted the industry. As AI technology continues to advance, we can expect to see even more innovative applications in the future. This presents a significant opportunity for academics and researchers to explore the potential of AI in entertainment and media and contribute to the growth of this exciting field.

AI-GENERATED ART & WRITING

The emergence of artificial intelligence has brought forth a new form of artistic creation: AI-generated art. This article critically examines the controversial issues surrounding AI-generated art, focusing on debates related to creativity, authorship, and aesthetic judgment. By exploring these contentious topics, we shed light on the complex relationship between AI and human artistic practices, and the implications for the future of art.

AI-generated art refers to artworks created or co-created by AI systems, utilizing machine learning algorithms and generative models. The proliferation of AI-generated art has sparked debates within the artistic community and broader society. This article delves into the controversies surrounding AI-generated art, aiming to explore the implications for creativity, authorship, and aesthetic judgment.

One of the primary concerns surrounding AI-generated art is the question of creativity. Critics argue that true creativity requires human consciousness, subjectivity, and the ability to imbue artworks with personal experiences and emotions. Proponents of AI-generated art, on the other hand, contend that AI systems can generate novel and innovative artistic expressions, challenging the traditional notions of human creativity. This debate raises profound philosophical questions about the nature of creativity and the role of human agency in artistic production.

AI-generated artworks often raise questions about authorship and the attribution of creative efforts. Who should be credited as the creator of an AI-generated artwork: the AI system, the human programmer, or both? This issue raises legal, ethical, and cultural dilemmas regarding ownership, intellectual property, and the recognition of artistic contributions. The blurring of authorship boundaries in AI-generated art challenges established conventions and prompts reevaluation of the concept of artistic authorship.

Assessing the aesthetic value of AI-generated art poses a significant challenge. How do we evaluate artworks created by non-human entities? Critics argue that AI-generated art lacks the depth, intentionality, and human experiences that underpin traditional artistic practices. The subjectivity of aesthetic judgment becomes increasingly complex when human preferences and biases are embedded in AI algorithms. The controversy surrounding the aesthetic judgment of AI-generated art underscores the need to redefine criteria for evaluating artistic quality in the context of AI.

The rise of AI-generated art raises broader cultural and social implications. Some argue that AI-generated art perpetuates the commodification of art and reinforces existing power structures by favoring established artists and institutions with access to AI technology. Others express concerns about the potential loss of human creativity and the erosion of the value of traditional artistic practices. Additionally, AI-generated art presents challenges in terms of cultural appropriation and the potential for biased or offensive creations.

The controversies surrounding AI-generated art are multifaceted, touching on fundamental aspects of human creativity, authorship, aesthetic judgment, and the societal value of art. The emergence of AI in the artistic domain prompts a reevaluation of established norms and conventions, challenging us to engage in nuanced discussions about the nature of creativity, the roles of humans and machines, and the cultural implications of AI-generated art. By critically examining these controversial issues, we can foster a deeper understanding of the complex relationship between AI and art, paving the way for ethical considerations, policy developments, and informed perspectives on the future of artistic creation.

AI-Generated Text

Artificial intelligence has revolutionized the generation of text, giving rise to an array of applications such as automated content creation, chatbots, and language models. However, the proliferation of AI-generated text has sparked significant controversy. This article critically examines the controversial issues surrounding AI-generated text, focusing on ethical concerns, challenges to authenticity, and the broader social implications of its widespread use. By addressing these contentious topics, we aim to shed light on the multifaceted dimensions of AI-generated text and foster informed discussions on its impact.

AI-generated text, powered by natural language processing algorithms, has disrupted traditional notions of authorship, creativity, and the veracity of information. The increased use of AI in generating written content has raised ethical, legal, and social questions. This article provides a comprehensive analysis of the controversial issues surrounding AI-generated text, exploring ethical considerations, challenges to authenticity, and the broader societal implications.

The ethical concerns surrounding AI-generated text are manifold. AI systems can be programmed to generate deceptive or misleading content, leading to issues of misinformation, propaganda, and malicious use. The lack of transparency regarding the origin of AI-generated text raises questions about accountability and responsibility. Ethical considerations also extend to issues such as privacy, data ownership, and the potential for AI to amplify existing biases and discriminatory language.

AI-generated text blurs the boundaries between human-generated and machine-generated content, challenging the notion of authenticity. With the ability to mimic human language patterns and styles, AI-generated text can be indistinguishable from human-written text, leading to challenges in verifying the origin and intent of a given piece of text. This raises concerns about trustworthiness, intellectual property, and the erosion of trust in information sources.

The proliferation of AI-generated text has disrupted traditional publishing and journalism industries. Automated content creation can produce vast quantities of text at unprecedented speeds, potentially replacing human writers and editors. This has significant implications for employment, the quality of written content, and the role of professional journalists. The devaluation of human labor in the writing process raises ethical questions about fair compensation and the impact on the integrity of journalism.

AI-generated text carries socio-cultural implications. The use of AI-generated text in social media, political campaigns, and public discourse raises concerns about the manipulation of public opinion and the erosion of trust in democratic processes. Additionally, the homogenization of content generated by AI systems may stifle diverse voices, creativity, and cultural expression. The social impact of AI-generated text highlights the need for responsible deployment, transparency, and regulation to mitigate potential harms.

AI-generated text poses legal and regulatory challenges. Copyright infringement, plagiarism, and intellectual property disputes become more complex when AI systems generate text. Determining liability for defamatory or harmful content generated by AI also raises legal questions. Existing legal frameworks may struggle to address the unique challenges posed by AI-generated text, necessitating the development of updated regulations and ethical guidelines.

The controversies surrounding AI-generated text encompass ethical considerations, challenges to authenticity, and broader social implications. The ethical concerns of AI-generated text extend beyond mere technological advancements, raising profound questions about the responsible use of AI, the preservation of authenticity, and the social impact on various industries. Addressing these controversies requires interdisciplinary collaboration among researchers, policymakers, and industry stakeholders. By navigating the complexities of AI-generated text, society can harness its potential benefits while mitigating its risks, fostering a balanced and ethically sound approach to the integration of AI in written communication.

THE FUTURE OF AI IN ENTERTAINMENT AND MEDIA

The entertainment and media industry has been transformed by the advancements in artificial intelligence technology. AI has enabled the creation of new forms of content, enhanced user experiences, and increased efficiency in various aspects of the industry.

With the rapid pace of technological advancement, it is important to understand the future directions of AI in entertainment and media.

AI-Powered Personalization

Personalization has become an essential aspect of the entertainment and media industry. AI algorithms can analyze user data and preferences to provide personalized content recommendations, music playlists, and movie suggestions. AI-powered personalization can help content providers to tailor their offerings to individual users, leading to increased engagement and retention.

AI-Generated Content

AI-generated content is an emerging trend in the entertainment and media industry. AI algorithms can generate content such as music, art, and even movies. AI-generated content has the potential to revolutionize the industry by reducing production costs and increasing the diversity of content available.

However, concerns have been raised about the potential impact on the creative process and the role of human creativity in the industry.

AI Enhanced User Experiences

AI technology can enhance user experiences by providing personalized recommendations, interactive content, and immersive experiences. AI-powered chatbots and virtual assistants can also improve customer service and support. The use of AI in entertainment and media is expected to increase as users demand more interactive and personalized experiences.

AI for Content Distribution

AI algorithms can analyze user behavior and preferences to optimize content distribution.

AI-powered content distribution can help content providers to reach their target audience more effectively and increase engagement and retention.

AI can also help to reduce piracy by identifying and removing unauthorized content.

Conclusion

The future of AI in entertainment and media is promising. AI technology has the potential to transform the industry by providing personalized content, reducing production costs, and enhancing user experiences.

However, it is important to consider the potential impact on the creative process and the role of human creativity in the industry. As the technology continues to evolve, it is imperative for the entertainment and media industry to stay informed and adapt to the changing landscape.

AI IN THE WORKPLACE

AI FOR HEALTHCARE

Artificial intelligence has revolutionized the healthcare industry in recent years, transforming the way medical professionals diagnose, treat, and manage diseases. The use of AI in healthcare has significantly improved patient outcomes, enhanced clinical decision-making, and reduced healthcare costs.

AI in healthcare involves the use of machine learning algorithms and deep learning neural networks to analyze vast amounts of medical data and provide insights that can help doctors make more informed decisions. This technology can be used to identify potential health risks, diagnose diseases at an early stage, and even predict patient outcomes.

One of the most significant benefits of AI in healthcare is its ability to analyze medical images such as X-rays, MRI scans, and CT scans. AI algorithms can detect even the slightest anomalies that may be missed by human radiologists, enabling early detection of diseases such as cancer. AI can also be used to monitor patients remotely, reducing the need for hospital visits and improving patient outcomes.

AI has also been used in drug discovery, where machine learning algorithms are used to analyze vast amounts of data to identify potential drug candidates. This technology has significantly reduced the time and cost involved in drug development, leading to the development of new treatments for diseases.

However, the use of AI in healthcare also raises concerns about data privacy and security.

Medical data is highly sensitive, and there is a risk of data breaches and cyber-attacks.

Therefore, it is essential to implement robust data protection measures to ensure the security and confidentiality of patient information.

AI has transformed the healthcare industry, improving patient outcomes and reducing healthcare costs. However, it is essential to address AI's ethical and legal implications in healthcare to ensure that patient data is protected and used ethically. The use of AI in healthcare is just the beginning, and we can expect to see further advancements and innovations in this field in the coming years.

AI-Based Diagnosis and Treatment

Artificial intelligence has revolutionized various fields, and healthcare is no exception.

The use of AI in healthcare has increased significantly in recent years, and it has proven to be an effective tool for diagnosing and treating various diseases. AI-based diagnosis and treatment is a promising approach that has the potential to transform healthcare and improve patient outcomes.

AI-based diagnosis and treatment involve the use of machine learning algorithms to analyze patient data and provide accurate diagnoses.

Machine learning algorithms can analyze vast amounts of data quickly and accurately, which makes them ideal for diagnosing complex diseases. AI-based diagnosis and treatment can also help physicians make more informed decisions about treatment options. By analyzing patient data, AI systems can provide personalized treatment recommendations tailored to each patient's specific needs.

One of the key benefits of AI-based diagnosis and treatment is its ability to improve patient outcomes. By providing more accurate diagnoses and personalized treatment recommendations, AI systems can help physicians provide better care to their patients. AI-based diagnosis and treatment can also reduce the risk of misdiagnosis and unnecessary treatments, which can lead to better patient outcomes and lower healthcare costs.

In addition to healthcare, AI-based diagnosis and treatment can also be applied to other fields, such as finance and banking, education and e-learning, customer service and support, cybersecurity and data protection, transportation and logistics, marketing and advertising, agriculture and farming, environmental sustainability, and entertainment and media.

For example, AI-based customer service and support can help companies provide better customer service by analyzing customer data and providing personalized recommendations.

AI-based cybersecurity and data protection can help protect sensitive data by identifying potential threats and taking proactive measures to prevent them. AI-based marketing and advertising can help companies target their ads more effectively by analyzing customer data and providing personalized recommendations.

AI-based diagnosis and treatment is a promising approach that can potentially transform healthcare and other fields. By analyzing vast amounts of data quickly and accurately, AI systems can provide more accurate diagnoses and personalized treatment recommendations, leading to better patient outcomes and lower healthcare costs. As AI continues to evolve, its potential applications in healthcare and other fields will continue to expand, making it an exciting area for research and innovation.

AI for Drug Discovery

AI for drug discovery is a rapidly growing field transforming how pharmaceutical companies develop new drugs. With the help of artificial intelligence, researchers can now more efficiently identify potential drugs that have the potential to be effective in treating a variety of diseases.

One of the most significant advantages of using AI in drug discovery is the ability to analyze vast amounts of data quickly and accurately. For example, pharmaceutical companies can use machine learning algorithms to sift through enormous databases of molecular structures and identify compounds that are most likely to have a therapeutic effect.

AI can also help researchers predict the safety and efficacy of potential drugs before they are tested in humans. By analyzing data from previous clinical trials and molecular and cellular data, AI algorithms can predict the likelihood of a drug being effective and identify potential side effects.

AI can also help researchers design new drugs that are more effective and have fewer side effects. By analyzing the molecular structure of existing drugs and identifying areas for improvement, AI algorithms can help researchers design drugs that are more targeted and have a higher likelihood of success.

Overall, AI has the potential to revolutionize drug discovery and development. By leveraging the power of machine learning, pharmaceutical companies can develop new drugs more efficiently and with a higher degree of accuracy. This will ultimately lead to the development of more effective treatments for a variety of diseases and improve the health and well-being of people around the world.

In conclusion, AI for drug discovery has the potential to transform the pharmaceutical industry and improve healthcare outcomes for millions of people. As AI technology continues to advance, we can expect to see even more significant breakthroughs in drug discovery and development, and the field of medicine as a whole.

AI for Clinical Trials

Artificial intelligence is rapidly gaining momentum in clinical trials. AI is revolutionizing the process of drug development and clinical trials in the healthcare industry. AI-powered clinical trials can help identify patients, design protocols, analyze data, and improve the trial's efficiency.

The primary benefit of using AI in clinical trials is the ability to analyze vast amounts of data quickly and accurately. AI algorithms can analyze and interpret data from multiple sources, including electronic health records, genetic data, and patient-generated data. This analysis can help researchers identify potential participants for a clinical trial, design the study protocol, and monitor the patients' progress during the trial.

AI can also help in reducing the cost and time required for clinical trials. The AI algorithms can optimize the trial design, identify potential risks, and improve the safety of the trial. AI can also help predict the trial's outcome, reducing the number of patients required to participate and shortening the trial duration.

Moreover, AI can help in improving the accuracy of clinical trial data. The AI algorithms can detect errors and inconsistencies in the data, reducing the risk of data manipulation or fraud. AI can also help improve patient engagement and retention in the trial, which is critical for the study's success.

AI is transforming the healthcare industry, and its application in clinical trials is no exception. AI-powered clinical trials can improve the trial's efficiency, accuracy, and safety, reducing the cost and time required for drug development. The use of AI in clinical trials has the potential to revolutionize the healthcare industry, bringing new treatments and cures to patients faster and more effectively than ever before.

Ethical and Legal Issues Related to AI in Healthcare

The use of artificial intelligence in healthcare has revolutionized the way medical professionals diagnose and treat patients. AI is being used to analyze medical images, predict disease outbreaks, and develop personalized treatment plans. However, the integration of AI in healthcare also poses ethical and legal challenges that must be addressed.

One of the primary ethical concerns is the potential for AI to perpetuate existing biases in healthcare. For example, if an AI algorithm is trained on data that is biased against certain groups, it may produce inaccurate or discriminatory results. Additionally, the use of AI raises questions about data privacy and informed consent. Patients must be informed of how their data will be used and have the right to opt-out of data collection.

The legal issues surrounding AI in healthcare are also complex. Liability is a major concern. If an AI system makes a mistake that results in harm to a patient, who is responsible? The manufacturer of the AI system, the healthcare provider who implemented it, or both? The lack of clear legal frameworks for AI in healthcare exacerbates these issues.

Moreover, the use of AI in diagnosis and treatment raises questions about the role of healthcare professionals. Will AI systems replace doctors and nurses altogether? It is unlikely, but the integration of AI may change the role of healthcare professionals significantly. They will need to be trained on how to use and interpret AI-generated data, and they must be prepared to collaborate with AI systems to provide the best possible care for patients.

In conclusion, the integration of AI in healthcare can potentially improve patient outcomes and revolutionize the healthcare industry. However, ethical and legal issues surrounding AI must be addressed to ensure that the technology is used responsibly and for the benefit of patients. It is essential that medical professionals, policymakers, and AI developers work together to create clear ethical and legal frameworks for the use of AI in healthcare.

AI FOR FINANCE AND BANKING

Artificial intelligence has become an integral part of the finance and banking industry. It has made significant strides in transforming the way financial institutions operate, making them more efficient, accurate, and reliable. AI has several applications in finance and banking, ranging from fraud detection to credit scoring, risk management, and investment analysis.

AI-powered chatbots and virtual assistants are now common in the banking industry, providing customers with quick and efficient customer service. These chatbots use natural language processing (NLP) to understand customer queries and provide appropriate responses. They also have the ability to carry out transactions, check account balances, and provide investment advice.

One of the significant benefits of AI in finance and banking is its ability to detect fraudulent activities. AI algorithms can analyze large volumes of data and identify patterns that indicate fraudulent transactions. This helps financial institutions prevent fraudulent activities and protect their customers' accounts.

AI also plays a vital role in credit scoring, which helps financial institutions assess borrowers' creditworthiness. AI algorithms analyze data such as credit history, income, and employment status to determine the risk associated with lending to a particular borrower. This helps financial institutions to make informed lending decisions and reduce the risk of default.

AI-powered risk management systems are also gaining popularity in the finance and banking industry. These systems can analyze market data and identify potential risks, enabling financial institutions to take preemptive measures to mitigate risks.

Finally, AI has also made significant strides in investment analysis. AI algorithms can analyze large volumes of data and identify trends and patterns that can help investors make informed investment decisions. This has led to the emergence of robo-advisors, which provide personalized investment advice to individual investors.

Overall, AI has transformed the finance and banking industry, making it more efficient, accurate, and reliable. Financial institutions that embrace AI are likely to gain a competitive advantage and provide better services to their customers.

AI for Fraud Detection and Prevention

AI for Fraud Detection and Prevention Fraud is a pervasive issue in various industries, including finance, banking, healthcare, and more. The advent of artificial intelligence has provided a powerful tool for detecting and preventing fraudulent activities. AI algorithms can analyze vast amounts of data, identify patterns, and ag suspicious transactions. This subchapter explores the potential of AI for fraud detection and prevention across different industries.

The financial sector is one of the primary targets of fraudsters. AI can help banks and financial institutions detect fraudulent activities in real-time by analyzing customers' transactions and behavior. AI can also identify anomalies in financial statements, detect unusual trading patterns, and prevent money laundering.

Fraud in healthcare can come in various forms, such as billing fraud, prescription fraud, and insurance fraud. AI can detect fraudulent activities in healthcare by analyzing medical claims, identifying patterns of fraudulent behavior, and tagging suspicious claims. AI can also improve patient safety by identifying potential fraud in medical prescriptions.

Fraud in Customer Service and Support

AI-powered chatbots can help companies detect and prevent fraudulent activities by identifying suspicious behavior during customer interactions. For example, chatbots can analyze customers' messages and identify patterns of fraudulent behavior, such as phishing attempts.

Fraud in Cybersecurity and Data Protection

AI algorithms can detect and prevent cyber threats by analyzing network traffic, identifying potential vulnerabilities, and predicting future attacks. AI can also help organizations identify fraudulent activities related to data breaches, such as unauthorized access to sensitive data.

Fraud in Transportation and Logistics

The transportation and logistics industry is vulnerable to fraud, such as cargo theft, invoice fraud, and identity theft. AI can help prevent these types of fraud by analyzing shipping data, identifying unusual patterns, and tagging suspicious activities.

Fraud in Marketing and Advertising

Fraud in marketing and advertising can come in various forms, such as click fraud, impression fraud, and ad stacking. AI can help detect and prevent fraud in marketing and advertising by analyzing online ad campaigns, identifying fraudulent activities, and blocking suspicious traffic.

Fraud in Agriculture

AI can help prevent fraud in agriculture and farming by analyzing agricultural data, identifying anomalies, and detecting fraudulent activities such as food adulteration, counterfeit seeds, and crop insurance fraud.

Fraud in Environmental Sustainability

AI can help prevent fraud in environmental sustainability by analyzing data related to carbon credits, identifying fraudulent activities, and increasing transparency in carbon markets.

Fraud in Entertainment Industries

AI can help prevent fraud in the entertainment and media industry by analyzing data related to digital rights management, identifying piracy, and protecting intellectual property.

AI has tremendous potential for detecting and preventing fraudulent activities across various industries. AI can help organizations reduce financial losses and maintain their reputation by identifying and preventing fraudulent activities in real-time.

However, ensuring that AI-powered fraud detection systems are transparent, ethical, and comply with relevant regulations is essential.

AI FOR RISK MANAGEMENT

Risk management is an essential aspect of decision-making in various industries. In the era of artificial intelligence, risk management has become more efficient and effective. AI algorithms can analyze vast amounts of data and provide accurate predictions and insights, enabling decision-makers to manage risks better.

Risk Management in Healthcare

AI is transforming the healthcare industry by providing valuable insights into patient care, drug development, and disease prevention.

AI-powered risk management solutions can identify potential risks in patient care, such as misdiagnosis or medication errors. The data generated by AI algorithms can be used to develop personalized treatment plans that minimize risks and improve patient outcomes.

Risk Management in Finance and Banking

The finance and banking industry is highly regulated, and risk management is a critical component of their business operations. AI-powered risk management solutions can analyze market trends, identify potential fraud, and detect anomalies in financial transactions.

AI algorithms can also predict the likelihood of loan defaults and identify potential investment opportunities.

Risk Management in Education and E-Learning

AI is transforming the education industry by providing personalized learning experiences and improving the efficiency of education delivery. AI-powered risk management solutions can analyze student data to identify potential risks, such as dropouts or academic underperformance. AI algorithms can also provide insights into student engagement and performance, enabling educators to develop personalized learning plans that minimize risks and improve student outcomes.

Risk Management in Customer Service

AI for Customer Service and Support AI-powered chatbots and virtual assistants are transforming customer service and support. AI algorithms can analyze customer data to identify potential risks, such as customer dissatisfaction or churn. AI-powered solutions can also provide personalized recommendations and support, enabling businesses to minimize risks and improve customer satisfaction.

Risk Management in Cybersecurity and Data Protection

Cybersecurity and data protection are critical issues in the digital age. AI-powered risk management solutions can analyze network traffic and identify potential security threats. AI algorithms can also detect data access and usage anomalies, enabling businesses to protect their data from potential breaches.

Risk Management in Transportation and Logistics

AI-powered risk management solutions are transforming the transportation and logistics industry by optimizing supply chain management and improving delivery times. AI algorithms can analyze traffic patterns, weather conditions, and other data to identify potential risks, such as delays or disruptions.

AI-powered solutions can also provide real-time updates and recommendations, enabling businesses to minimize risks and improve efficiency.

Risk Management in Marketing and Advertising

AI algorithms can analyze customer data and provide valuable insights into consumer behavior and preferences. AI-powered risk management solutions can identify potential risks in marketing and advertising campaigns, such as low engagement or ad fraud. AI-powered solutions can also provide personalized recommendations and support, enabling businesses to minimize risks and improve campaign effectiveness.

Risk Management in Agriculture and Farming

AI-powered risk management solutions are transforming the agriculture and farming industry by providing valuable insights into crop management and disease prevention. AI algorithms can analyze weather patterns, soil conditions, and other data to identify potential risks, such as crop failure or disease outbreaks.

AI-powered solutions can also provide personalized recommendations and support, enabling farmers to minimize risks and improve crop yields.

Risk Management in Environmental Sustainability

AI algorithms can analyze environmental data and provide valuable insights into climate change and sustainability. AI-powered risk management solutions can identify potential risks, such as pollution or deforestation. AI-powered solutions can also provide personalized recommendations and support, enabling businesses and governments to minimize risks and improve sustainability.

Risk Management in Entertainment and Media

AI-powered risk management solutions are transforming the entertainment and media industry by providing valuable insights into audience behavior and preferences. AI algorithms can analyze social media data, viewer ratings, and other data to identify potential risks, such as low engagement or negative reviews. AI-powered solutions can also provide personalized recommendations and support, enabling businesses to minimize risks and improve content effectiveness.

AI-powered risk management solutions are transforming various industries by providing valuable insights into potential risks and enabling decision-makers to make more informed decisions. The integration of AI algorithms into risk management strategies is essential in the era of AI, and businesses that adopt these solutions will have a significant competitive advantage.

AI for Investment Analysis and Decision-Making

Artificial intelligence is rapidly changing the world of investment analysis and decision-making. The use of AI in finance and banking is growing at an unprecedented rate, with more and more financial institutions adopting AI technologies to streamline their processes and improve their investment decisions. AI-powered investment analysis and decision-making tools can help investors identify opportunities, assess risks, and make better investment decisions. These tools use machine learning algorithms to analyze vast amounts of data, including market trends, financial reports, news articles, and social media feeds, to identify patterns and trends that humans may not be able to detect.

One of the key benefits of AI-powered investment analysis and decision-making is the ability to make more informed decisions in real-time. This is particularly important in the fast-paced world of finance and banking, where decisions need to be made quickly to take advantage of changing market conditions.

AI can also help investors manage risk more effectively by identifying potential risks and providing early warning signals of potential problems. This can help investors make more informed decisions about when to buy or sell a particular asset, and can help them avoid costly mistakes.

Another crucial benefit of AI-powered investment analysis and decision-making is the ability to personalize investment advice and recommendations. By analyzing a client's financial data, investment history, and risk tolerance, AI can provide personalized investment advice that is tailored to their specific needs and goals.

However, the use of AI in investment analysis and decision-making is not without its challenges. One of the biggest challenges is the need for high-quality data. AI algorithms rely on large amounts of data to make accurate predictions, so it is essential that the data used is accurate and up-to-date.

In addition, there is a risk that AI-powered investment analysis and decision-making tools could lead to over-reliance on technology and the automation of decision-making. This could lead to a loss of human judgment and intuition, which could negatively affect investors.

Despite these challenges, the use of AI in investment analysis and decision-making is set to continue to grow in the coming years.

As AI technologies continue to evolve and improve, they will become an increasingly important tool for investors looking to make better, more informed investment decisions.

Ethical and Legal Issues Related to AI in Finance and Banking

As artificial intelligence continues to permeate various industries, it is becoming increasingly important to address the ethical and legal issues related to its use in finance and banking. While AI has the potential to revolutionize the financial sector, it also poses significant ethical and legal challenges.

One of the main ethical concerns related to AI in finance and banking is the potential for algorithmic bias. AI algorithms are only as unbiased as the data they are trained on, and if the data is biased, then the algorithm will be too. This can lead to discriminatory outcomes, such as denying loans or other financial services to certain groups of people based on their race or gender. To mitigate this risk, it is essential to ensure that AI algorithms are trained on diverse and representative data sets and are regularly audited for bias.

Another ethical issue related to AI in finance and banking is the potential for job loss. As AI becomes more prevalent in the financial sector, it may replace human workers in certain roles, such as customer service and data entry. This could have significant economic and social implications, and it is vital for policymakers and industry leaders to consider ways to mitigate the impact on workers.

From a legal standpoint, there are also several issues to consider when it comes to AI in finance and banking. One of the main concerns is data privacy and security. AI algorithms rely on vast amounts of data to make predictions and decisions, and if this data is not properly secured, it can be vulnerable to cyber-attacks and other security breaches. It is important for financial institutions to implement robust data protection measures and comply with relevant data privacy regulations.

Another legal issue related to AI in finance and banking is transparency and accountability. AI algorithms can be opaque and difficult to understand, which can make it difficult to determine how they are making decisions and whether they are complying with relevant regulations. There is a need for greater transparency and accountability in developing and using AI algorithms in the financial sector.

Overall, while AI has the potential to revolutionize the financial sector, it is important to address the ethical and legal issues related to its use in finance and banking. By doing so, we can ensure that AI is developed and used in a responsible and ethical manner that benefits society as a whole.

AI FOR EDUCATION AND
E-LEARNING

AI is transforming the education industry, and e-learning is at the forefront of this change. AI has the potential to personalize education, make it more accessible, and improve learning outcomes. In this chapter, we will provide an overview of AI in education and e-learning.

One of the most significant advantages of AI in education is that it can personalize learning to meet individual students' needs. AI algorithms can analyze student data and create personalized learning paths that are tailored to each student's strengths and weaknesses. This approach ensures that students receive the right level of challenge and support, which can improve their engagement and learning outcomes.

Another advantage of AI in education is that it can make education more accessible. AI-powered tools such as chatbots and virtual assistants can provide students with instant support and guidance, reducing the need for face-to-face interactions.

This is especially important for students who have disabilities or live in remote areas with limited access to educational resources.

AI can also help educators save time and improve their teaching effectiveness. For example, AI-powered grading systems can analyze student work and provide instant feedback, reducing the time educators spend on manual grading. AI-powered tutoring systems can also provide students with immediate feedback and guidance, allowing educators to focus on more complex tasks such as lesson planning and curriculum development.

There are, of course, challenges associated with AI in education. One of the biggest challenges is ensuring that AI-powered systems are unbiased and fair. AI algorithms can replicate and even amplify existing biases and inequalities, which can have negative consequences for students. It is essential to design AI systems that are transparent and accountable to ensure that they do not perpetuate existing inequalities.

In conclusion, AI is transforming the education industry, and e-learning is at the forefront of this change. AI has the potential to personalize education, make it more accessible, and improve learning outcomes. However, to realize these benefits, it is essential to design AI systems that are unbiased, transparent, and accountable.

AI-Based Personalized Learning

AI-based personalized learning is an emerging trend in the field of education and e-learning. With the advent of AI, the traditional one-size-fits-all approach to education is becoming obsolete. AI-based personalized learning is a powerful tool that can help educators tailor their teaching to the individual needs of each student.

AI-based personalized learning uses sophisticated algorithms to analyze student performance data and identify areas where students need more help or where they are excelling. It can also take into account a student's learning style, personality, and interests to create a customized learning experience that is engaging and effective.

AI-based personalized learning has the potential to revolutionize education and e-learning. It can help students learn at their own pace, in their own way, and on their own schedule. This can lead to better academic performance, higher student engagement, and improved retention.

AI-based personalized learning is not just limited to the classroom. It can also be used in other areas such as healthcare, finance, banking, customer service and support, cybersecurity and data protection, transportation and logistics, marketing and advertising, agriculture and farming, environmental sustainability, and entertainment and media.

For example, AI-based personalized learning can be used in healthcare to create customized treatment plans for patients based on their medical history, genetic makeup, and lifestyle. In finance and banking, it can be used to create personalized investment portfolios based on an individual's risk tolerance and financial goals. In customer service and support, AI-based personalized learning can help companies provide better customer service by tailoring their support to each customer's individual needs.

In cybersecurity and data protection, AI-based personalized learning can help organizations identify and respond to threats based on the unique characteristics of their systems and networks. In transportation and logistics, it can be used to optimize routes and schedules based on real-time data and individual customer needs. In marketing and advertising, AI-based personalized learning can help companies create targeted campaigns based on individual customer preferences and behaviors.

Overall, AI-based personalized learning is a powerful tool that can help educators and organizations provide better services to their customers and stakeholders. As AI technology continues to evolve, we can expect to see even more innovative applications of AI-based personalized learning in the future.

AI for Student Assessment and Evaluation

AI for student assessment and evaluation is a rapidly growing field that utilizes machine learning and data analytics to improve the accuracy and efficiency of grading processes.

With the ability to analyze vast amounts of data, AI can provide valuable insights into student performance, identify areas of weakness, and help educators tailor their teaching methods to better meet the needs of each student.

One of the most significant benefits of AI in student assessment is its ability to reduce bias and increase fairness in grading. Traditional grading methods are often subjective, and studies have shown that students from certain demographics are more likely to receive lower grades than others. AI algorithms, on the other hand, are designed to be impartial and objective, ensuring that all students are evaluated fairly.

Another advantage of AI in student assessment is its ability to provide immediate feedback to both students and educators.

With the use of machine learning algorithms, AI can quickly analyze student work and provide real-time feedback on areas that need improvement. This helps students identify and correct their mistakes and allows educators to adjust their teaching methods and provide more personalized instruction.

AI can also be used to analyze student behavior and engagement, providing insights into how students learn and interact with educational materials. By tracking student progress and performance over time, AI can help educators identify patterns and trends in student behavior, allowing them to make more informed decisions about how to best support their students.

However, it is important to note that AI is not a panacea for all educational challenges. While AI can provide valuable insights and support, it is not a substitute for human interaction and judgment. Educators must be careful to ensure that AI is used in ways that align with their pedagogical goals and values, and that students are not reduced to mere data points.

Overall, AI for student assessment and evaluation has the potential to revolutionize the way we think about teaching and learning.

By leveraging the power of machine learning and data analytics, educators can gain deeper insights into student performance and provide more personalized instruction, ultimately leading to better outcomes for all students.

AI for Curriculum Design and Development

Artificial intelligence has revolutionized the way we live, work, and learn. The technology has found its way into various industries, including education and e-learning. AI for curriculum design and development is a rapidly growing field that promises to transform how we approach education.

Curriculum design and development is a critical aspect of education. It is the process of creating and implementing educational programs that meet the needs of students and align with the goals of the institution.

Traditionally, curriculum design and development have been the responsibility of educators and academic experts. However, with the advent of AI, this process is becoming more automated and data-driven.

AI can help educators create personalized learning experiences for students. By analyzing student performance and behavior data, AI algorithms can identify areas where students are struggling and provide targeted interventions to help them improve.

This approach can help educators tailor their teaching to the individual needs of each student, rather than relying on a one-size- fits-all approach.

AI can assist educators develop more engaging and effective learning materials. By analyzing data on student engagement and performance, AI algorithms can identify which materials are most effective and which ones need improvement. This approach can help educators create more engaging and interactive learning materials tailored to their students' needs.

AI can also help educators track student progress and provide feedback. AI algorithms can provide real-time feedback to students and educators by analyzing data on student performance and behavior. This approach can help educators identify areas where students are struggling and provide targeted interventions to help them improve.

In conclusion, AI for curriculum design and development is a rapidly growing field that promises to transform the way we approach education. By using AI algorithms to analyze data on student performance and behavior, educators can create personalized learning experiences that are tailored to the individual needs of each student. This approach can help educators create more engaging and effective learning materials and provide real-time feedback to students and educators. As AI continues to evolve, it will undoubtedly play an increasingly important role in the future of education.

Ethical and Legal Issues Related to AI in Education and e-Learning

Artificial intelligence has the potential to revolutionize the field of education and e-learning, making it more accessible, personalized, and effective. However, as with any technological innovation, there are ethical and legal issues that need to be addressed to ensure that AI is used responsibly and ethically.

One of the critical ethical concerns related to AI in education is the potential for bias and discrimination. AI algorithms are only as unbiased as the data they are trained on, and if this data reflects existing biases and prejudices, the AI system will perpetuate them. For example, an AI-powered educational platform that recommends careers based on gender stereotypes could reinforce gender inequalities.

Another ethical issue related to AI in education is the use of data and privacy. AI systems often collect large amounts of data about students, including their academic performance, behavior, and personal information. This data can be used to improve the system's effectiveness, but it also raises concerns about privacy and data protection. Students and their parents need to be informed about what data is collected, how it is used, and who has access to it.

In addition to ethical concerns, there are also legal issues related to AI in education and e-learning. For example, there are laws and regulations that govern data protection and privacy, such as the General Data Protection Regulation (GDPR) in Europe. Educational institutions must ensure that they comply with these laws when using AI systems that collect and process personal data.

Another legal issue related to AI in education is intellectual property. AI systems can be used to create educational content, such as textbooks and online courses. However, there are questions about who owns the copyright to this content, especially if AI algorithms generate it.

Overall, the use of AI in education and e-learning has the potential to transform the way we learn and teach. However, to ensure that AI is used responsibly and ethically, it is important to address the ethical and legal issues related to its use. Educational institutions and policymakers need to work together to develop guidelines and regulations that promote the responsible use of AI in education.

AI FOR CUSTOMER
SERVICE AND SUPPORT

Artificial intelligence is transforming the way businesses interact with their customers. With advancements in natural language processing, machine learning, and other AI technologies, customer service and support are becoming more efficient, effective, and personalized. In this chapter, we will explore the impact of AI on customer service and support, its benefits, challenges, and future prospects.

AI is being used in various ways to enhance customer service and support. Chatbots, virtual assistants, and voice assistants are some of the popular AI applications in customer support. These AI-powered tools can handle routine queries, respond instantly, and direct customers to the right resources. They can also learn from customer interactions, identify patterns, and improve their performance over time. AI can also be used for sentiment analysis, which helps businesses understand their customers' emotions and preferences. This information can be used to personalize the customer experience, recommend products and services, and improve customer satisfaction.

Benefits of AI in Customer Service and Support

AI has several benefits for customer service and support. It can reduce the workload of human agents, automate routine tasks, and provide instant responses to customers. This can result in faster resolution times, reduced wait times, and improved customer satisfaction. AI can also provide 24/7 support, which is not possible with human agents alone. This can help businesses provide better customer service and support, even outside regular working hours. AI also enables businesses to collect and analyze large amounts of customer data, which can be used to improve products and services, identify new market opportunities, and enhance customer experiences.

Challenges of AI in Customer Service and Support

Despite its benefits, AI also poses some challenges for customer service and support.

One of the biggest challenges is the lack of human touch. While AI can provide instant responses, it cannot replicate the empathy and emotional intelligence of human agents.

This can result in customers feeling frustrated or dissatisfied with the service. Another challenge is the potential for bias in AI algorithms. If not properly designed and trained, AI algorithms can perpetuate biases and discrimination, which can harm customers and damage brand reputation. Finally, AI requires significant investment in infrastructure, software, and talent, which may not be feasible for all businesses.

Future Prospects of AI in Customer Service and Support

The future of AI in customer service and support looks promising. AI technologies are evolving rapidly, with new applications and capabilities being developed every day. As AI becomes more sophisticated, businesses can expect to see even more benefits, such as improved personalization, advanced analytics, and enhanced security. However, to fully realize the potential of AI, businesses must also address the challenges, such as bias and lack of empathy. By doing so, they can create a customer service and support experience that is efficient, effective, and personalized.

AI-Based Chatbots and Virtual Assistants

AI-based chatbots and virtual assistants are becoming increasingly popular across various industries, ranging from healthcare, finance, education, customer service and support, cybersecurity and data protection, transportation and logistics, marketing and advertising, agriculture and farming, and environmental sustainability to entertainment and media.

The rise of AI-based chatbots and virtual assistants can be attributed to their numerous benefits. First and foremost, they enhance customer experience by providing 24/7 support, assistance, and personalized services. Moreover, they are cost-effective, efficient, and scalable, as they can handle multiple requests simultaneously and reduce human errors and response times.

In the healthcare industry, AI-based chatbots and virtual assistants enable patients to access medical advice, diagnosis, and treatment recommendations remotely, thereby improving access and equity in healthcare. In finance and banking, they allow customers to conduct transactions, manage accounts and access financial advice without physical interaction with bank staff, thereby reducing costs and improving efficiency.

In education and e-learning, AI-based chatbots and virtual assistants can enhance personalized learning experiences, providing students with customized learning paths, feedback, and support. They can also facilitate student-teacher interactions, making learning more engaging and interactive.

In customer service and support, AI-based chatbots and virtual assistants can handle routine customer queries and requests, freeing up human staff to focus on more complex issues. They can also provide personalized recommendations and services, based on customer preferences and history.

In cybersecurity and data protection, AI-based chatbots and virtual assistants can detect and respond to security threats and breaches, thereby enhancing data privacy and protection.

In transportation and logistics, AI-based chatbots and virtual assistants can provide real-time updates and recommendations on transport schedules, routes, and traffic conditions, thereby improving efficiency and reducing delays.

In marketing and advertising, AI-based chatbots and virtual assistants can facilitate personalized and targeted marketing campaigns based on customer data and preferences.

In agriculture and farming, AI-based chatbots and virtual assistants can provide real-time monitoring and management of crop growth, soil conditions, and weather patterns, thereby optimizing crop fields and reducing resource waste.

In environmental sustainability, AI-based chatbots and virtual assistants can facilitate the monitoring and managing of environmental data, such as air and water quality, waste management, and energy consumption, enabling more effective and sustainable environmental policies and practices.

In entertainment and media, AI-based chatbots and virtual assistants can enhance user engagement and interaction, by providing personalized recommendations, feedback, and content based on user preferences and history.

Overall, AI-based chatbots and virtual assistants offer numerous benefits across various industries, enhancing customer experiences, improving efficiency and scalability, and enabling more effective and sustainable practices and policies. However, their adoption and implementation require careful consideration of ethical, legal, and social implications, and ongoing research and innovation to ensure their effectiveness and sustainability.

AI for customer feedback analysis AI for customer feedback analysis is a powerful tool for businesses to gain insights into their customer's opinions, preferences, and experiences. With the rise of social media and online reviews, customer feedback has become increasingly important in shaping a company's reputation and success. AI can help businesses analyze and understand this feedback in real-time, allowing them to make data-driven decisions and improve their customer service.

One way AI can be used for customer feedback analysis is through sentiment analysis. This technique involves using natural language processing to analyze customer reviews and social media posts to determine the sentiment behind them. By identifying keywords and phrases, AI can determine whether a customer's feedback is positive, negative, or neutral. This information can then be used to identify trends and areas for improvement.

Another way AI can be used for customer feedback analysis is through topic modeling.

This technique involves using machine learning algorithms to identify common topics and themes in customer feedback. By grouping similar feedback together, businesses can gain a better understanding of what their customers are saying about their products or services. This information can then be used to improve products or services or to tailor marketing campaigns.

AI can also be used for predictive analysis, allowing businesses to anticipate customer needs and preferences. By analyzing customer data and behavior, AI can predict what a customer is likely to purchase or what type of support they may need. This information can then be used to personalize marketing campaigns or provide targeted customer support.

AI for customer feedback analysis is a valuable tool for businesses looking to improve their customer service and reputation. By analyzing customer feedback in real-time, businesses can identify trends and make data-driven decisions to improve their products, services, and customer experiences. As AI technology continues to advance, it is likely that its applications in customer feedback analysis will become even more powerful and effective.

AI for Customer Experience Management

AI for customer experience management has become a popular trend in the business world today. It has revolutionized how companies interact with their customers and has helped improve customer satisfaction, engagement, and loyalty. With the help of AI, companies can now offer personalized experiences to their customers, enhance their brand reputation, and increase their revenue.

In the field of customer service and support, AI-powered chatbots and virtual assistants are now widely used by companies to provide 24/7 support to their customers. These chatbots are programmed to answer frequently asked questions, provide product recommendations, and even resolve customer complaints. They can also be integrated with other systems like CRM and ERP to provide a seamless experience to customers.

In the entertainment and media industry, AI is used to personalize customer content. With the help of machine learning algorithms, companies can now analyze customer data to understand their preferences and offer personalized recommendations. This has led to an increase in customer engagement and loyalty, as customers feel that the company understands their needs and preferences.

In the finance and banking industry, AI is being used to detect fraud and improve security. With the help of machine learning algorithms, banks can now analyze customer data to detect fraudulent activities and prevent them before they happen. This has helped to reduce the risk of financial losses and improve customer trust.

In the field of healthcare, AI is being used to improve patient care and outcomes. With the help of machine learning algorithms, doctors can now analyze patient data to predict diseases, develop personalized treatment plans, and monitor patient progress. This has led to improved patient outcomes and reduced healthcare costs.

In conclusion, AI has opened up new possibilities for customer experience management across various industries. It has helped companies improve customer satisfaction, engagement, and loyalty while increasing their revenue. As AI technology continues to evolve, we can expect to see even more innovation in this field in the coming years.

Ethical and Legal Issues in Customer Service and Support

As artificial intelligence continues to advance and become integrated into various aspects of our lives, including customer service and support, ethical and legal issues arise.

These issues must be addressed to ensure that AI is used in a manner that is fair, unbiased, and transparent.

One of the primary ethical concerns with AI in customer service and support is the potential for bias. AI algorithms are only as unbiased as the data they are trained on. If the data used to train an AI system is biased, then the system will also be biased. This could result in discriminatory practices, such as denying service to certain individuals or groups based on factors such as race or gender.

Another ethical issue related to AI in customer service is privacy. AI technologies can collect vast amounts of personal data from customers, including their browsing history, purchase history, and personal preferences.

This data must be handled with care to ensure that customer privacy is protected.

Legal issues also arise with the use of AI in customer service and support. For example, there may be concerns around liability if an AI system makes a mistake that causes harm to a customer. Additionally, there may be regulatory requirements that need to be met to ensure that AI systems are used in a compliant manner.

To address these ethical and legal issues, it is important for companies to be transparent about how they are using AI in their customer service and support operations. They should also ensure that the data used to train AI systems is diverse and unbiased. Additionally, companies should have clear policies in place around data privacy and security.

Overall, while AI has the potential to revolutionize customer service and support, it is important to ensure that it is used in an ethical and legal manner. By addressing these issues, we can create a future where AI is used to enhance customer experiences in a fair and transparent way.

AI FOR CYBERSECURITY AND DATA PROTECTION

Artificial intelligence has revolutionized several industries, and cybersecurity and data protection are no exceptions. AI has transformed the way organizations protect their data and networks from cyber threats. It has also enhanced the detection and mitigation of cyber-attacks and enabled better risk management.

AI in cybersecurity and data protection involves the use of machine learning algorithms and other AI technologies to identify and respond to cyber threats. These technologies can analyze vast amounts of data and identify patterns that may indicate a potential attack. They can also detect and respond to threats in real-time, reducing the response time to cyber incidents.

One of the primary benefits of AI in cybersecurity and data protection is improved threat detection. Traditional security solutions rely on known signatures or patterns of cyber attacks. However, AI-based solutions can identify previously unknown threats and adapt to new attack patterns. This is particularly useful in detecting advanced persistent threats (APTs) that are designed to evade traditional security measures.

AI can also automate the process of risk management and compliance. Organizations can use AI to monitor their networks and systems continuously, identify vulnerabilities and prioritize remediation efforts. They can also use AI to ensure compliance with regulatory requirements and industry standards.

AI is also useful in enhancing incident response. AI-based solutions can analyze data from multiple sources and provide real-time insights into the nature and severity of a cyber attack. This enables security teams to respond quickly and effectively to mitigate the impact of the attack.

In conclusion, AI has transformed cybersecurity and data protection, enabling organizations to detect and respond to cyber threats more effectively. With the increasing sophistication of cyber attacks, AI-based solutions will become even more critical in protecting organizations' critical information and networks.

AI for Threat Detection and Prevention

In recent years, the use of artificial intelligence has become increasingly popular in various industries. One area where AI has proven particularly useful is in threat detection and prevention. As technology advances and the world becomes more reliant on digital systems, the need for effective cybersecurity measures has become more pressing. This is where AI can play a significant role.

AI for threat detection and prevention involves using algorithms and machine learning techniques to identify potential threats and take action to mitigate them. This can include analyzing network traffic to identify suspicious activity, scanning for malware and viruses, and using behavioral analysis to detect anomalies in user activity. AI can also help with incident response, allowing security teams to quickly identify and respond to threats.

In the healthcare industry, AI can be used to detect and prevent threats such as medical identity theft and data breaches. AI-powered cybersecurity solutions can also help hospitals and healthcare providers comply with strict regulations around patient data protection.

In finance and banking, AI can be used to detect fraudulent transactions and prevent financial fraud. AI powered fraud detection systems can analyze large amounts of data and identify patterns that may indicate fraudulent behavior.

In education and e-learning, AI can help prevent cheating and academic dishonesty.

AI-powered plagiarism detection tools can scan student papers and assignments for copied content, helping to maintain academic integrity.

In customer service and support, AI can help prevent fraud and identity theft by identifying suspicious activity and verifying customer identities. AI-powered chatbots can also help customers with security-related issues, such as resetting passwords and reporting suspicious emails.

In transportation and logistics, AI can help prevent accidents and improve safety. AI-powered sensors can monitor vehicles and detect potential issues before they become a problem.

In marketing and advertising, AI can help prevent fraud and improve targeting. AI-powered fraud detection systems can identify fake clicks and impressions, while AI-powered advertising platforms can use data analysis to improve ad targeting and optimize campaigns.

AI can help prevent crop damage and improve yields in agriculture and farming. AI-powered sensors can monitor soil moisture levels and detect pest infestations, allowing farmers to take action before crops are damaged.

In environmental sustainability, AI can help prevent pollution and protect natural resources. AI-powered sensors can monitor air and water quality, while AI-powered analytics can help identify areas where conservation efforts are most needed.

AI can help prevent piracy and protect intellectual property in entertainment and media. AI-powered content recognition tools can identify copyrighted material and prevent it from being illegally distributed.

Overall, AI for threat detection and prevention has the potential to revolutionize cybersecurity across a wide range of industries.

As technology continues to advance, it is likely that AI will play an increasingly important role in keeping our digital systems safe and secure.

AI for Identity and Access Management

Identity and access management (IAM) is a crucial aspect of any organization's security framework. It involves managing and controlling access to sensitive data and resources based on user identity and privileges. In the era of AI, IAM is becoming more sophisticated, providing organizations with enhanced security and convenience.

AI-powered IAM systems use machine learning algorithms to analyze user behavior and identify potential security threats. These systems can detect anomalies in user behavior, such as unusual login times or locations, and flag them for further investigation. By automating these processes, AI can reduce the workload on security teams and improve the accuracy of threat detection.

AI algorithms can also help with identity verification. Biometric authentication, such as facial recognition and fingerprint scanning, is becoming more prevalent in IAM systems. AI can analyze these biometric data points to ensure that the person attempting to access a resource is who they claim to be. This can improve security while also providing a more convenient user experience.

Another area where AI is making a significant impact on IAM is in password management.

Passwords are a common weak point in security, as they can be easily guessed or stolen. AI-powered password management systems can analyze user behavior and generate unique, complex passwords that are much harder to crack. These systems can also detect when a password has been compromised and prompt the user to change it.

AI for IAM is not without its challenges. Privacy concerns around biometric data and user behavior tracking need to be carefully addressed. Additionally, the use of AI in IAM requires significant resources and expertise, making it less accessible to small businesses.

Despite these challenges, the benefits of AI-powered IAM are clear. Organizations can improve their security posture by automating threat detection and identity verification while providing a better user experience. As AI continues to evolve, we can expect to see even more innovation in this area.

AI for Data Privacy and Protection

Artificial intelligence is changing the way we live and work, and it has also become an important tool for data privacy and protection.

In an era where data is becoming increasingly valuable, it is critical to have adequate data protection measures in place. AI can help organizations to improve their data privacy and protection efforts by identifying potential threats and vulnerabilities, and taking proactive steps to mitigate them.

In healthcare, AI is particularly useful for data privacy and protection. With the growing use of electronic health records and other digital healthcare technologies, it is essential to safeguard sensitive patient information. AI can help healthcare organizations to detect and prevent potential data breaches by monitoring access to patient records and identifying unusual activity.

AI can help healthcare organizations to comply with privacy regulations, such as HIPAA, by identifying areas of non-compliance and providing recommendations for improvement.

In the finance and banking industry, AI can help to detect and prevent fraud, which is a major concern for many organizations. By analyzing large amounts of data, AI algorithms can identify patterns and anomalies that may indicate fraudulent activity, such as unusual transactions or account access from unfamiliar locations. This can help banks and other financial institutions to quickly respond to potential threats and prevent financial losses.

In the education and e-learning industry, AI can help to protect student data and improve learning outcomes. By analyzing student performance data, AI algorithms can identify areas of strength and weakness, and provide personalized recommendations for improvement. Additionally, AI can help to protect student data by monitoring access to learning materials and identifying potential security breaches.

In the customer service and support industry, AI can help organizations to improve their response times and provide better customer experiences. By analyzing customer data, AI algorithms can identify common issues and provide automated responses, freeing up customer service representatives to focus on more complex issues. Additionally, AI can help to protect customer data by monitoring access to customer records and identifying potential breaches.

In the cybersecurity and data protection industry, AI can help to detect and prevent cyber-attacks. By analyzing network traffic and system logs, AI algorithms can identify potential threats and take proactive steps to prevent them. Additionally, AI can help organizations to comply with data protection regulations by identifying areas of non-compliance and providing recommendations for improvement.

In the transportation and logistics industry, AI can help to improve supply chain efficiency and protect sensitive data. By analyzing shipping data, AI algorithms can identify potential delays or disruptions and provide recommendations for improvement.

Additionally, AI can help to protect sensitive data by monitoring access to shipping records and identifying potential security breaches.

In the marketing and advertising industry, AI can help to improve targeting and personalization efforts while protecting customer data. AI algorithms can identify customer preferences and provide targeted recommendations by analyzing customer data.

AI can help to protect customer data by monitoring access to marketing records and identifying potential breaches.

In the agriculture and farming industry, AI can help to improve crop yields and protect sensitive data. By analyzing weather data and soil conditions, AI algorithms can provide recommendations for optimal planting and harvesting times. Additionally, AI can help to protect sensitive data by monitoring access to crop records and identifying potential security breaches.

In the environmental sustainability industry, AI can help to improve conservation efforts and protect sensitive data. By analyzing environmental data, AI algorithms can identify areas of concern and provide recommendations for improvement.

AI can also help to protect sensitive data by monitoring access to environmental records and identifying potential security breaches.

In the entertainment and media industry, AI can help to improve content creation and protect sensitive data. By analyzing audience data, AI algorithms can identify trends and preferences, and provide recommendations for content creation. Additionally, AI can help to protect sensitive data by monitoring access to media records and identifying potential security breaches.

AI is an essential tool for data privacy and protection in a variety of industries. By analyzing large amounts of data and identifying potential threats, AI can help organizations to improve their data protection efforts and comply with privacy regulations. As AI continues to evolve, we can expect to see even more innovative uses for this technology in data privacy and protection.

Ethical and legal issues related to AI in cybersecurity and data protection

Artificial Intelligence has revolutionized the way we live, work, interact, and engage with each other. From healthcare to finance, education to customer service, and transportation to marketing, AI has made significant contributions in many fields.

However, with the increasing use of AI in cybersecurity and data protection, ethical and legal issues have emerged that need to be addressed.

The use of AI in cybersecurity and data protection has raised concerns about privacy, security, and transparency. AI algorithms can process vast amounts of data, detect anomalies, and identify potential threats, making it a valuable tool for protecting sensitive information. However, the use of AI in this context also raises concerns about potential bias, discrimination, and misuse of data.

One of the ethical issues related to AI in cybersecurity and data protection is the potential for bias and discrimination. AI algorithms are trained using historical data, which may contain biases or reject existing societal inequalities. This can result in discriminatory outcomes, such as the targeting of certain groups or individuals based on their race or gender.

Another ethical issue related to AI in cybersecurity and data protection is the lack of transparency. AI algorithms are often complex and difficult to understand, making it challenging to determine how they make decisions. This can lead to a lack of accountability, as it may be challenging to identify how and why a decision was made.

From a legal perspective, the use of AI in cybersecurity and data protection raises questions about liability and responsibility.

Who is responsible if an AI system makes a mistake or causes harm? Is it the developer, the user, or the AI system itself? These complex legal questions need to be addressed as AI becomes more prevalent in cybersecurity and data protection.

In conclusion, the use of AI in cybersecurity and data protection has significant potential for improving security and protecting sensitive information. However, it also raises ethical and legal issues that need to be addressed. To ensure that AI is used ethically and responsibly in this context, it is critical to promote transparency, accountability, and fairness in developing and deploying AI systems. Only then can we fully realize the benefits of AI in cybersecurity and data protection while minimizing the risks.

AI FOR TRANSPORTATION AND LOGISTICS

Artificial intelligence is transforming the transportation and logistics industry by enhancing operational efficiency, reducing costs, and improving customer experience. AI has numerous applications in this sector, including route optimization, demand forecasting, supply chain management, and autonomous vehicles.

Route Optimization

AI technology can optimize delivery routes by considering factors such as traffic, weather, and road conditions. This saves time and reduces fuel costs, which ultimately translates to cost savings for logistics companies. Real-time data analysis can also help logistics companies identify and mitigate bottlenecks in their supply chain.

Demand Forecasting

Demand forecasting is essential for logistics companies to manage inventory and ensure timely delivery to customers. AI algorithms can analyze data from various sources, including historical sales data and social media activity, to predict demand accurately. This helps companies to optimize their inventory levels and avoid stockouts.

Supply Chain Management

AI can streamline supply chain management by automating processes such as order processing, shipment tracking, and inventory management. This reduces the risk of errors and delays, improves efficiency, and ultimately enhances customer satisfaction.

Autonomous Vehicles

Autonomous vehicles are a key application of AI in transportation and logistics. These vehicles are equipped with sensors and AI algorithms that enable them to navigate roads and highways without human intervention.

Autonomous vehicles can reduce the risk of accidents, increase efficiency, and improve delivery times.

AI is revolutionizing the transportation and logistics industry by enabling companies to optimize their operations, reduce costs, and enhance customer experience. The applications of AI in this sector are diverse, ranging from route optimization to autonomous vehicles. As AI technology continues to evolve, we can expect to see more innovations in the transportation and logistics industry.

AI for Route Optimization and Planning

AI for route optimization and planning is a crucial application of AI in the transportation and logistics industry. With the increasing demand for faster, cheaper, and more efficient transportation of goods and services, AI offers a promising solution to the challenges of route optimization and planning.

AI algorithms can help in predicting traffic patterns, weather conditions, and other factors that affect the transportation of goods and services. This can help in optimizing the routes and reducing the delivery time, which is critical for businesses that rely on timely delivery of their products.

In the healthcare industry, AI can be used to optimize the routes of medical supplies and equipment, making it easier for healthcare professionals to access the necessary resources, especially in rural areas. This can help in improving the quality of healthcare delivery and reduce the mortality rate.

In the finance and banking industry, AI can be used to optimize the routes of cash delivery, reducing the risks associated with cash transportation. This can help improve the financial system's security and reduce the costs associated with cash transportation.

In the education and e-learning industry, AI can be used to optimize the routes of educational resources, making it easier for students to access the necessary resources, especially in remote areas. This can help in improving the quality of education delivery and reduce the dropout rate.

In the customer service and support industry, AI can be used to optimize the routes of customer support agents, making it easier for them to access the necessary resources and provide timely support to customers. This can help in improving customer satisfaction and loyalty.

In the cybersecurity and data protection industry, AI can be used to optimize the routes of data centers, reducing the risks associated with data transportation. This can help in improving the security of the data and reducing the costs associated with data transportation.

In the agriculture and farming industry, AI can be used to optimize the routes of agricultural resources, making it easier for farmers to access the necessary resources and improve crop yield. This can help in improving the efficiency of the agriculture industry and reducing food wastage.

In the environmental sustainability industry, AI can be used to optimize the routes of waste disposal, reducing the environmental impact of transportation and improving the sustainability of the environment.

In the entertainment and media industry, AI can be used to optimize the routes of media resources, making it easier for media professionals to access the necessary resources and improve the quality of media content. This can help in improving the entertainment experience for consumers and increasing the revenue of the entertainment industry.

In conclusion, AI for route optimization and planning offers a promising solution to transportation and logistics challenges. Its applications in various industries can help in improving efficiency, reducing costs, and improving the quality of services. As researchers and academics, it is important to continue exploring the potential of AI in this field and to develop new solutions that can help in addressing the evolving needs of businesses and society.

AI for Fleet Management and Maintenance

Managing and maintaining a fleet of vehicles can be a complex and challenging task. Fleet managers need to ensure that their vehicles are in good condition, serviced regularly, and driven safely. However, with the advent of AI, fleet management and maintenance have become much easier and more efficient.

AI-powered solutions can help fleet managers to optimize their operations, reduce costs, and improve safety. For instance, predictive maintenance using AI algorithms can identify potential vehicle issues before they become serious problems. This can help fleet managers to schedule maintenance proactively, thus avoiding costly breakdowns and reducing downtime.

Moreover, AI can also help fleet managers to optimize their routes and schedules, reducing fuel consumption and improving the efficiency of their operations. AI algorithms can analyze traffic patterns, weather conditions, and other factors to identify the most efficient routes for each vehicle in the fleet.

AI can also significantly improve driver safety. AI-powered solutions can monitor driver behavior in real-time, detecting risky driving habits such as speeding, harsh braking, and distracted driving. This can help fleet managers to identify drivers who need additional training and coaching to improve their driving skills.

In conclusion, AI has the potential to revolutionize fleet management and maintenance. By leveraging the power of AI, fleet managers can optimize their operations, reduce costs, improve safety, and provide better service to their customers. As such, it is essential for fleet managers to embrace AI and explore the various solutions available to them.

AI for Supply Chain Management

Supply chain management is a complex process involving various activities, from planning and forecasting to procurement, production, and logistics. The use of AI in supply chain management can revolutionize how organizations manage their supply chain operations, making them more efficient, cost-effective, and responsive to changing market demands.

AI-driven supply chain management can help organizations optimize their inventory levels, reduce lead times, improve demand forecasting accuracy, and enhance supply chain visibility. With AI, organizations can analyze vast amounts of data to identify patterns and trends, and make better-informed decisions about their supply chain operations.

One of the key benefits of AI in supply chain management is the ability to automate routine tasks, such as inventory management and order processing. This reduces the workload on human employees and minimizes the risk of errors and delays, resulting in faster and more accurate fulfillment of customer orders.

AI can also help organizations respond more quickly to supply chain disruptions, such as natural disasters or supplier bankruptcies. By analyzing real-time data from multiple sources, AI can identify potential risks and provide recommendations for alternative suppliers or transportation routes.

In the agriculture and farming industry, AI can help optimize crop yields and reduce waste by analyzing weather patterns, soil conditions, and other environmental factors. AI can also help identify potential pest infestations and provide recommendations for effective pest control measures.

In the transportation and logistics industry, AI can optimize delivery routes, reduce fuel consumption, and improve driver safety by analyzing traffic patterns, weather conditions, and other factors that affect transportation operations.

In the entertainment and media industry, AI can help personalize content recommendations and improve audience engagement by analyzing user data and preferences. AI can also help optimize advertising campaigns by analyzing audience behavior and identifying the most effective marketing channels.

Overall, AI has the potential to transform supply chain management across a range of industries, making operations more efficient, cost-effective, and responsive to changing market demands. As organizations continue to adopt AI-driven supply chain management solutions, it is important to ensure that these solutions are designed and implemented to balance the benefits of AI with the need to protect the privacy and security of sensitive data.

Artificial Intelligence has become increasingly popular in different sectors, including transportation and logistics. AI has brought about a lot of benefits, such as improving efficiency, reducing costs, enhancing safety, and making transportation more environmentally friendly. However, the use of AI in transportation and logistics also raises serious ethical and legal issues that must be addressed.

One of the major ethical concerns related to AI in transportation and logistics is the potential loss of jobs. As AI systems become more advanced, they may replace human workers, leading to unemployment and economic instability. This issue needs to be addressed by creating new job opportunities and providing training for workers to adapt to the new technology.

Another ethical issue is the potential for AI systems to make decisions that could harm humans or the environment. For instance, an autonomous vehicle may have to make a decision about whether to swerve to avoid hitting a pedestrian or stay on course and collide with the pedestrian. Such decisions raise ethical questions about who should be held responsible for the outcome and how such decisions should be made.

The legal issues related to AI in transportation and logistics are also significant. For instance, there are concerns about liability in case of accidents involving autonomous vehicles.

Who is responsible for accidents caused by such vehicles? Is it the manufacturer, the owner, or the AI system itself? The legal framework needs to be updated to address these issues.

Another legal issue is data privacy and protection. AI systems in transportation and logistics generate vast amounts of data that need to be stored and processed. This data may contain sensitive information, such as personal and financial data. Companies need to ensure that such data is stored and processed securely to prevent unauthorized access or misuse.

In conclusion, the use of AI in transportation and logistics has brought about significant benefits, but it also raises serious ethical and legal issues.

Companies and policymakers need to address these issues to ensure that the benefits of AI are realized while minimizing the negative consequences.

AI FOR MARKETING
AND ADVERTISING

Artificial intelligence has been a game-changer in the world of marketing and advertising. As businesses strive to stay ahead of the competition, they increasingly turn to AI-powered solutions to better understand their customers, tailor their marketing strategies, and improve their overall effectiveness.

In marketing and advertising, AI has been used in various ways, such as predictive analytics, natural language processing, machine learning, and computer vision. These technologies have enabled marketers to analyze large amounts of data, gain insights into consumer behavior, and personalize their marketing campaigns to specific audiences.

For example, AI-powered chatbots have transformed customer service and support, enabling businesses to offer 24/7 assistance to customers and automate routine tasks. In addition, AI algorithms can analyze customer data to predict future behavior, enabling marketers to tailor their messaging and offers to individual consumers.

AI has also revolutionized digital advertising, with programmatic advertising allowing for real-time bidding and optimization of ads based on user behavior. AI algorithms can analyze user data to identify the most effective ad placements and ad formats, leading to higher engagement rates and better ROI for advertisers.

In the realm of e-commerce, AI-powered recommendation engines have become a critical tool for businesses looking to upsell and cross-sell products to customers. These engines use machine learning algorithms to analyze user behavior and recommend relevant products, leading to higher conversion rates and increased revenue.

However, with the increasing use of AI in marketing and advertising comes the need for careful consideration of ethical concerns such as privacy, bias, and transparency. As AI algorithms become more sophisticated, it is important for businesses to ensure that they are being used responsibly and not perpetuating harmful stereotypes or discriminating against certain groups of consumers.

Overall, AI has the potential to transform the way we approach marketing and advertising, enabling businesses to gain a deeper understanding of their customers and deliver more personalized experiences. However, it is important for businesses to use these technologies responsibly and ethically to ensure that they are not doing harm.

AI for Customer Segmentation and Targeting

One of the most significant advantages of using AI in marketing and advertising is the ability to segment and target customers effectively. With AI-powered tools, businesses can analyze vast amounts of customer data to identify patterns, preferences, and behaviors. This information can be used to create highly personalized and targeted marketing campaigns that resonate with customers on a deeper level.

Customer segmentation involves dividing customers into groups based on shared characteristics like age, gender, location, interests, and purchasing behavior. With AI, businesses can go beyond these basic demographics and create more sophisticated segments based on factors such as online behavior, social media activity, emotions, and personality traits.

Once customers are segmented, businesses can use AI to target them with tailored messaging and offers that are more likely to convert. This can be done through a variety of channels, including email, social media, and digital advertising. By delivering personalized and relevant content, businesses can improve customer engagement and loyalty, increase sales, and grow their customer base.

In the entertainment and media industry, AI can be particularly useful for customer segmentation and targeting. With so many different types of content and platforms available, it can be challenging to determine which content will resonate with which audiences. AI-powered tools can help identify trends and patterns in customer behavior, allowing businesses to create and promote content that is more likely to be successful.

For example, Netflix uses AI algorithms to recommend movies and TV shows to its users based on their viewing history and preferences. This improves the user experience and helps Netflix retain customers and increase revenue.

In summary, AI is a powerful tool for customer segmentation and targeting. By leveraging the vast amounts of data available, businesses can create more sophisticated segments and deliver personalized content that resonates with customers on a deeper level. In the entertainment and media industry, AI can help businesses create and promote content that is more likely to be successful, ultimately leading to increased engagement, loyalty, and revenue.

AI for Personalized Advertising

Artificial intelligence is revolutionizing the way we approach advertising and marketing. By leveraging machine learning algorithms and big data analytics, businesses can now create personalized advertising campaigns that are tailored to individual preferences and interests. This improves the effectiveness of advertising campaigns and enhances customer experience and engagement.

AI-powered personalized advertising has become increasingly popular in recent years, particularly in the retail and e-commerce industries. By analyzing customer data such as browsing history, search queries, and purchase behavior, AI algorithms can create targeted advertisements that are more likely to resonate with customers. For example, an online clothing store can use AI to recommend products to customers based on their previous purchases and browsing history, increasing the likelihood of a sale.

AI is also being used in the healthcare industry for personalized advertising campaigns. By analyzing patient data, healthcare providers can create targeted advertisements for specific medical treatments or services. This improves patient outcomes and helps healthcare providers reach their target audience more effectively.

In the finance and banking industry, AI is being used to personalize advertising campaigns for financial products and services. By analyzing customer data such as income, spending habits, and credit history, banks, and financial institutions can create targeted advertising campaigns that are more likely to resonate with customers and lead to more sales.

AI is also being used in education and e-learning to create personalized advertising campaigns for online courses and educational programs. By analyzing student data such as learning styles and interests, AI algorithms can create targeted advertisements that are more likely to attract students and increase enrollment.

In customer service and support, AI-powered chatbots are being used to improve customer experience and engagement. Chatbots can help businesses increase customer satisfaction and loyalty by analyzing customer queries and providing personalized responses.

AI is also being used in cybersecurity and data protection to create personalized advertising campaigns for security products and services.

By analyzing customer data such as online behavior and security risks, AI algorithms can create targeted advertisements for specific security products that are more likely to resonate with customers.

In transportation and logistics, AI is being used to create personalized advertising campaigns for transportation services. By analyzing customer data such as travel history and preferences, AI algorithms can create targeted advertisements that are more likely to attract customers and increase sales.

AI-powered personalized advertising is also being used in agriculture and farming to create targeted advertisements for agricultural products and services. By analyzing data such as weather patterns and crop yields, AI algorithms can create targeted advertisements that are more likely to resonate with farmers and increase sales.

AI is also being used in environmental sustainability to create personalized advertising campaigns for sustainable products and services. By analyzing customer data such as environmental values and preferences, AI algorithms can create targeted advertisements that are more likely to resonate with customers and promote sustainable practices.

In the entertainment and media industry, AI is being used to create personalized advertising campaigns for movies, TV shows, and music.

By analyzing customer data such as viewing history and preferences, AI algorithms can create targeted advertisements that are more likely to attract viewers and increase revenue.

In conclusion, AI is transforming the advertising and marketing industry by allowing businesses to create personalized advertising campaigns tailored to individual preferences and interests. This improves the effectiveness of advertising campaigns and enhances customer experience and engagement. As AI technology continues to evolve, we can expect to see even more innovative uses of AI in personalized advertising across a range of industries and niches.

AI for Campaign Optimization and Measurement

The use of artificial intelligence in campaign optimization and measurement has revolutionized the way businesses approach marketing and advertising. AI algorithms can analyze large amounts of data to identify patterns and trends that can help marketers optimize their campaigns to reach their target audience more effectively.

One way that AI is used in campaign optimization is through the use of predictive modeling. Predictive models use algorithms to analyze historical data and predict future outcomes. By analyzing past campaigns and customer behavior, marketers can use predictive modeling to make informed decisions about future campaigns and optimize them for better results.

Another way that AI is used in campaign optimization is through the use of machine learning. Machine learning algorithms can analyze customer behavior and preferences to identify patterns and trends that can help marketers optimize their campaigns for maximum impact. By using machine learning, marketers can create personalized campaigns that are tailored to the needs and interests of their target audience.

AI is also used in campaign measurement to track and analyze campaign performance. AI algorithms can analyze data in real-time to track campaign performance and identify areas for improvement. By using AI for campaign measurement, marketers can make informed decisions about future campaigns and optimize them for better results.

In addition to campaign optimization and measurement, AI is also used in other marketing and advertising areas. For example, AI is used to create personalized content and recommendations for customers, identify and target potential customers, and automate customer support and service.

Overall, using AI in campaign optimization and measurement has transformed how businesses approach marketing and advertising. By using AI algorithms to analyze data and identify patterns and trends, marketers can optimize their campaigns for better results and create personalized experiences for their target audience. As AI continues to evolve, we can expect to see even more innovative uses of AI in marketing and advertising in the future.

Ethical and Legal Issues Related to AI in Marketing and Advertising

As artificial intelligence continues to revolutionize various industries, it has also raised ethical and legal concerns in marketing and advertising. With the increasing use of AI in advertising, it is essential to address the ethical and legal issues that arise from the use of this technology.

One of the ethical concerns related to AI in marketing and advertising is the potential for AI to manipulate consumer behavior. AI algorithms can analyze consumer data and create personalized advertisements that are tailored to the individual's interests and preferences. While this can be seen as a positive development, it can also be used to manipulate consumers into making purchases they may not necessarily need or want.

Another ethical issue is the potential for AI to perpetuate biases. AI algorithms are designed to learn from data, and if the data is biased, the algorithm will learn and perpetuate those biases. This can result in discriminatory advertising that reinforces stereotypes and excludes certain groups.

From a legal perspective, there are concerns about data privacy and protection. AI algorithms rely on vast amounts of data to function effectively, and this data can include personal information such as browsing history, location data, and purchasing habits. As such, there is a risk of data breaches and misuse of consumer data, which could lead to legal rami cations.

Furthermore, there is a risk of AI-generated content infringing on copyright or trademark laws. As AI becomes more sophisticated, it is possible for it to create content that is similar to existing content, which could result in legal disputes.

To address these ethical and legal issues, it is important for marketers and advertisers to be transparent about their use of AI and its implications. It is also essential to ensure that AI algorithms are designed with ethical considerations in mind, such as avoiding biases and protecting consumer privacy.

In conclusion, while AI has the potential to transform marketing and advertising, it is crucial to address the ethical and legal issues that arise from its use. By being transparent and designing AI algorithms with ethical considerations in mind, we can ensure that AI is used responsibly and benefits businesses and consumers.

AI FOR AGRICULTURE
AND FARMING

Artificial intelligence is rapidly transforming the agricultural industry, providing innovative solutions to age-old problems. The use of AI in agriculture and farming has the potential to revolutionize the way we produce food, making it more efficient, sustainable, and cost-effective.

One of the primary applications of AI in agriculture is precision farming. This involves using sensors, drones, and other AI-powered technologies to collect data on soil quality, crop growth, and weather patterns. This data can then be used to optimize crop yields, reduce waste, and minimize the use of pesticides and fertilizers.

AI can also be used to automate various tasks in agriculture, such as planting, harvesting, and irrigation. This saves time and labor costs and reduces the risk of human error. Additionally, AI-powered robots can be used to perform tasks that are dangerous or difficult for humans, such as working in extreme weather conditions or handling hazardous chemicals.

Another area where AI is making a significant impact is in livestock farming. AI-powered systems can monitor animal behavior and health, detect diseases early, and optimize feeding and breeding programs. This can lead to improved animal welfare, increased productivity, and reduced environmental impact.

In addition to these practical applications, AI is also helping to address broader challenges in agriculture, such as climate change and food security. For example, AI can be used to predict weather patterns and monitor the impact of climate change on crops. It can also be used to analyze data on global food production and consumption, helping to identify areas where food shortages are likely to occur.

Overall, the use of AI in agriculture and farming is still in its early stages, but the potential benefits are enormous. As new technologies are developed and adopted, we can expect to see even more innovative solutions to the challenges facing the agricultural industry.

AI for Crop Monitoring and Management

Agriculture and farming have been revolutionized in recent years with the advent of AI technologies. AI has proved to be a game-changer in crop monitoring and management, helping farmers make informed decisions that can increase yield and improve crop quality.

AI can help farmers in several ways, such as detecting pests, predicting weather patterns, and monitoring crop growth. With AI-powered drones and satellites, farmers can get real-time data on crop conditions, soil moisture, and nutrient levels. This data is then analyzed using machine learning algorithms to provide insights that can help farmers optimize crop health and yield.

One of the most significant benefits of AI in agriculture is its ability to detect and prevent crop diseases and pests. By analyzing plant health and growth data, AI algorithms can detect early signs of disease or infestation, allowing farmers to take action before it spreads. This can save farmers significant losses in crop yield and quality, as well as reduce the need for harmful pesticides and chemicals.

AI can also help farmers optimize their water usage and reduce waste. By analyzing data on soil moisture, weather patterns, and crop growth, AI can provide farmers with insights on when and how much to water their crops.

This can help farmers save water and reduce their environmental impact.

Moreover, AI can provide farmers with insights into crop pricing and market trends, enabling them to make informed decisions on when to harvest and sell their crops. This can help farmers maximize their profits and reduce waste.

AI has proven to be a valuable tool for crop monitoring and management, enabling farmers to make informed decisions that can increase yield, improve crop quality, and reduce waste. As AI technologies continue to evolve, we can expect even more significant benefits for the agriculture industry, ultimately leading to a more sustainable and efficient food production system.

AI for Yield Prediction and Optimization.

The use of artificial intelligence in agriculture and farming has significantly improved crop yields and optimized resource use. With the help of AI, farmers can predict the yield of their crops and optimize their farming practices to maximize their harvests.

AI for yield prediction involves the use of machine learning algorithms that analyze various data points such as weather patterns, soil quality, and past crop yields to predict the outcome of the current crop. This technology helps farmers make informed decisions about when to plant, fertilize, and harvest their crops, resulting in better yields and increased pro ts.

Similarly, AI for yield optimization involves the use of machine learning models to optimize farming practices such as irrigation, fertilizer application, and pest control. By analyzing data such as soil moisture levels and weather patterns, AI can help farmers reduce resource waste and increase crop yields.

AI for agriculture and farming has the potential to revolutionize the industry, leading to increased food production and improved food security. With the global population projected to reach 9.7 billion by 2050, the need for sustainable and efficient agriculture practices is more critical than ever.

Moreover, AI for agriculture and farming has significant implications for environmental sustainability. By optimizing resource use and reducing waste, AI can help reduce the environmental impact of agriculture while still meeting the increasing demand for food.

In conclusion, AI for yield prediction and optimization is a critical application of AI in agriculture and farming. By leveraging machine learning algorithms to analyze data and optimize farming practices, farmers can increase their yields and reduce resource waste, leading to more sustainable and profitable agriculture practices.

AI for Livestock Monitoring and Management

The use of artificial intelligence in agriculture and farming has been gaining traction in recent years. One area that has seen significant progress is livestock monitoring and management. With the growing demand for meat, milk, and other animal products, farmers are increasingly turning to technology to improve efficiency and productivity while reducing costs.

AI-powered livestock monitoring and management systems can provide real-time data on individual animals' health, behavior, and productivity or entire herds. This data can be used to make informed decisions about feeding, breeding, and medical treatment, leading to improved animal welfare, higher yields, and reduced losses.

One example of AI for livestock monitoring and management is the use of sensors and cameras to track animals' movements and behavior. These sensors can detect changes in activity levels, feed intake, and even body temperature, allowing farmers to identify potential health issues before they become serious.

Another area where AI can make a significant impact is in disease detection and prevention.

By analyzing data from sensors, cameras, and other sources, AI algorithms can identify patterns and anomalies that may indicate the presence of disease. This information can be used to implement targeted interventions, such as quarantining infected animals or adjusting feed and water supplies.

AI can also help farmers optimize feed and water usage, reducing waste and maximizing efficiency. By analyzing data on animal behavior and environmental conditions, AI algorithms can recommend adjustments to feeding schedules and quantities, ensuring animals receive the right nutrients at the right time.

Finally, AI-powered livestock monitoring and management systems can help farmers comply with regulations and standards related to animal welfare and food safety. By providing detailed data on animal health and behavior, farmers can demonstrate compliance and avoid penalties.

Overall, AI for livestock monitoring and management has the potential to revolutionize the farming industry, improving animal welfare, increasing productivity, and reducing costs. As the technology continues to evolve, we can expect to see even more innovative solutions that address the unique challenges of farming and agriculture.

Ethical and Legal Issues Related to AI in Agriculture and Farming

As the use of artificial intelligence in various industries continues to grow, the agricultural and farming sector is not left behind. AI is now being used in agriculture and farming to improve crop yields, reduce costs, and increase efficiency. However, as with any new technology, ethical and legal issues arise, and it is essential to consider these issues to ensure the responsible use of AI in agriculture and farming.

One of the main ethical issues related to AI in agriculture is privacy. The use of AI in agriculture generates large amounts of data, including crop yields, soil data, and weather patterns. This data can be sensitive, and farmers must ensure that it is safeguarded.

Farmers must also be transparent about how they use this data and provide clear privacy policies to their customers.

Another ethical issue is the potential displacement of farm workers. AI can automate many tasks, and this could lead to job losses. It is essential to ensure that AI is used to complement human labor rather than replace it. This can be achieved by providing training and education to farmers and farm workers to enable them to work alongside AI systems.

The legal issues related to AI in agriculture are similar to those in other industries. These include issues around liability, accountability, and responsibility. For example, if a crop fails due to a malfunction in an AI system, who is liable for the loss? Is it the farmer, the software provider, or the manufacturer of the hardware?

It is important to ensure that legal frameworks are in place to address these issues.

In conclusion, the use of AI in agriculture and farming has the potential to revolutionize the sector. However, it is essential to consider the ethical and legal issues to ensure that AI is used responsibly. Farmers must be transparent about how they use data and provide clear privacy policies. They must also ensure that AI is used to complement human labor rather than replace it. Legal frameworks must also be in place to address liability and accountability issues. By considering these issues, we can ensure that AI in agriculture and farming is used for the benefit of all.

AI FOR ENVIRONMENTAL SUSTAINABILITY

The use of artificial intelligence in environmental sustainability is a growing trend that has the potential to revolutionize the way we address environmental challenges.

AI can be utilized to analyze large amounts of data, predict and prevent environmental disasters, optimize resource management, and even reduce carbon emissions. This subchapter will provide an overview of AI in environmental sustainability, including its applications and potential benefits.

One of the most significant applications of AI in environmental sustainability is predictive analysis. By analyzing historical data, AI algorithms can predict future environmental occurrences such as natural disasters, pollution levels, and climate change. This information can be used to develop strategies to prevent or mitigate the impact of these events. For example, AI-powered models can help predict the spread of forest fires and enable fire fighting teams to respond more effectively.

Another application of AI in environmental sustainability is resource optimization. AI can analyze data from various sources, such as weather patterns, soil quality, and water usage to optimize resource management. This information can be used to develop strategies that reduce waste and increase efficiency. For example, AI-powered irrigation systems can optimize the use of water in agriculture, reducing water usage and improving crop yields.

AI can also be used to reduce carbon emissions. AI algorithms can analyze energy usage data and develop strategies to reduce energy consumption. For example, AI-powered smart grids can optimize energy usage and reduce energy waste, resulting in lower carbon emissions.

In conclusion, AI has the potential to revolutionize the way we address environmental challenges. AI can help prevent environmental disasters and optimize resource management by analyzing large amounts of data and developing predictive models. Furthermore, AI can help reduce carbon emissions, contributing to the fight against climate change. As AI technology continues to evolve, we can expect to see more innovative applications of AI in environmental sustainability.

AI for Climate Change Mitigation and Adaptation

Climate change is one of the most pressing challenges facing the world today. It is causing significant changes to our environment, from rising sea levels and melting glaciers to more frequent extreme weather events. To mitigate the effects of climate change and adapt to its impacts, we need innovative solutions that can help us reduce greenhouse gas emissions and build resilience to its effects. AI can play a crucial role in this effort, offering a range of tools and technologies that can help us address the challenge of climate change in new and innovative ways.

One of the most promising applications of AI for climate change mitigation is in the field of energy management. AI algorithms can analyze data from energy systems to optimize their performance, reducing energy waste and improving efficiency. This can help reduce greenhouse gas emissions by lowering the amount of energy needed to power our homes and businesses.

AI can also be used to improve the accuracy of climate modeling and prediction. By analyzing large data sets and running complex simulations, AI algorithms can help us better understand the causes and impacts of climate change. This can help inform policy decisions and guide investments in infrastructure and adaptation measures.

AI can also be used to improve the resilience of communities and ecosystems to the impacts of climate change. By analyzing data on weather patterns and environmental factors, AI algorithms can help us identify areas that are most vulnerable to climate change and develop strategies to protect them. This can include everything from designing more resilient infrastructure to planting trees and other vegetation to absorb carbon dioxide from the atmosphere.

In the entertainment and media industry, AI can be used to raise awareness about climate change and encourage people to take action.

By using AI-powered tools to create more engaging and interactive content, media companies can help educate the public about the impacts of climate change and inspire them to take action.

AI has the potential to be a powerful tool for climate change mitigation and adaptation. By leveraging the power of AI to analyze data, develop models, and make predictions, we can develop innovative solutions that help us reduce greenhouse gas emissions, build resilience, and protect our planet for future generations. As academics and researchers, it is our responsibility to continue exploring the potential of AI in this field and to work together to develop new and innovative solutions to the challenge of climate change.

AI for Natural Resource Management

Natural resource management is a critical aspect of human life, and its proper management is crucial for sustainable development. Many organizations and individuals are involved in managing natural resources, such as land, water, forests, and wildlife. The effective management of these resources requires a lot of data analysis, planning, and decision-making, which can be time-consuming and complex. With the help of artificial intelligence, however, natural resource management can be made more efficient and effective.

AI is a powerful tool that can be used to analyze large amounts of data and provide insights that can help with decision-making.

For example, AI can be used to analyze satellite images and identify changes in land use patterns. This information can then be used to identify areas where land use is changing rapidly, which can help with conservation efforts. Similarly, AI can be used to analyze data on water quality, which can help identify areas where water pollution is a problem, and appropriate measures can be taken to address it.

AI can also be used to monitor wildlife populations. For instance, AI can help identify areas where certain species are at risk of extinction, and appropriate measures can be taken to protect them. AI can also help identify areas where poaching is taking place, and appropriate measures can be taken to prevent it.

In agriculture, AI can help with crop management. AI can be used to analyze soil data, weather patterns, and other factors that affect crop growth. This information can then be used to optimize crop yields, reduce waste, and improve overall efficiency.

AI can also be used to monitor and manage forests. AI can help identify areas where deforestation is taking place, and appropriate measures can be taken to prevent it. AI can also help identify areas where forest res are likely to occur, and appropriate measures can be taken to prevent them.

In conclusion, AI has the potential to revolutionize natural resource management.

Its ability to analyze large amounts of data and provide insights can help with decision-making and improve overall efficiency. As the world faces increasing environmental challenges, AI can play a critical role in helping to manage our natural resources sustainably.

AI for Waste Management and Recycling

AI has become a game-changer in many industries, including waste management and recycling. With the increasing amount of waste generated globally, it is essential to find innovative ways of managing and recycling waste. AI technology has proven to be a valuable tool in achieving these goals, and its potential is limitless.

One of the primary benefits of AI in waste management and recycling is its ability to optimize waste sorting and recycling processes. With AI-powered waste sorting systems, recycling facilities can sort waste more efficiently and accurately. These systems use sensors and cameras to identify and sort different types of waste, such as plastics, paper, and metal, which can then be recycled or reused.

AI can also help reduce waste by predicting and preventing waste generation. With predictive analytics, waste management companies can forecast waste generation patterns and develop strategies to reduce waste and improve recycling rates. AI algorithms can accurately predict waste generation patterns by analyzing data from various sources, such as weather patterns and consumer behavior.

Moreover, AI can help improve waste collection and transportation processes. With AI-powered waste collection and routing systems, waste management companies can optimize their collection routes to reduce fuel consumption and emissions. These systems also ensure that waste is collected on time and efficiently transported to the appropriate recycling facilities.

AI can also help improve the quality of recycled materials by identifying and removing contaminants from the recycling stream. With AI-powered quality control systems, recycling facilities can detect and remove contaminants, such as non-recyclable plastics and metals, from the recycling stream, ensuring that only high-quality recycled materials are produced.

In conclusion, AI has the potential to revolutionize waste management and recycling. With its ability to optimize waste sorting and recycling processes, predict and prevent waste generation, improve waste collection and transportation processes, and improve the quality of recycled materials, AI can help us achieve a more sustainable and circular economy. It is essential for academics and researchers to explore the potential of AI in waste management and recycling as innovative solutions to the world's waste management challenges.

Ethical and legal issues related to AI in environmental sustainability The use of Artificial Intelligence in environmental sustainability is a trending topic in many research and innovation circles.

AI technology is being leveraged to address some of the environmental challenges faced by the world today. However, the incorporation of AI in environmental sustainability raises ethical and legal concerns that need to be addressed.

One ethical issue associated with using AI in environmental sustainability is the possibility of creating a digital divide. The use of AI technology may create a divide between those with access to advanced technology and those without access. It may also widen the gap between developed and developing countries. This issue needs to be addressed to ensure that the benefits of AI technology are accessible to everyone.

Another ethical issue is the potential for AI to be misused. This could lead to unintended environmental consequences. For example, AI systems may be programmed to prioritize economic gains over environmental sustainability. This could lead to the exploitation of natural resources and the degradation of the environment.

The legal issues related to AI in environmental sustainability include data protection and privacy concerns. As AI systems collect and analyze large amounts of data, there is a risk of data breaches and misuse of personal data.

This could lead to legal issues related to data protection and privacy.

There are also legal issues related to liability and accountability. In the event of an environmental disaster caused by an AI system, it may be difficult to determine who is liable for the damage caused. This issue needs to be addressed to ensure that the responsible parties are held accountable.

In conclusion, the use of AI in environmental sustainability is a promising area of research and innovation. However, ethical and legal issues need to be addressed to ensure that the benefits of AI technology are accessible to everyone and that unintended environmental consequences are avoided. It is vital for academics and researchers to work together to find solutions to these issues and ensure that AI technology is used responsibly in environmental sustainability.

IMPLICATIONS OF AI FOR ACADEMICS AND RESEARCHERS

The emergence of artificial intelligence has opened up new avenues for research and innovation across various fields, including entertainment and media. As academics and researchers, it is essential to keep abreast of the latest developments in AI and explore its potential implications for different niches.

Below are some of the implications of AI for various sectors that researchers and academics need to consider.

AI for Healthcare: AI has the potential to revolutionize healthcare by enabling faster and more accurate diagnosis, improving patient outcomes, and reducing costs. As researchers, it is crucial to explore the ethical and legal implications of using AI in healthcare and investigate ways to ensure data privacy and security.

AI for Finance and Banking: AI has already disrupted the finance sector by automating routine tasks, providing personalized services, and identifying patterns that humans might miss. Researchers need to explore the implications of AI on financial stability, customer trust, and regulatory frameworks.

AI for Education and E-learning: AI has the potential to transform education by personalizing learning, improving student engagement, and providing real-time feedback. As researchers, it is essential to investigate the impact of AI on learning outcomes, student privacy, and teacher roles and responsibilities.

AI for Customer Service and Support: AI-powered chatbots and virtual assistants are already transforming customer service and support by providing faster and more personalized responses. Researchers need to explore the ethical implications of using AI in customer service and support and investigate ways to ensure transparency and accountability.

AI for Cybersecurity and Data Protection: AI has the potential to enhance cybersecurity by detecting and responding to threats in real-time, but it also poses new challenges for data protection and privacy. Researchers need to explore the implications of AI for cybersecurity and investigate ways to ensure data privacy and security.

AI for Transportation and Logistics: AI has the potential to optimize transportation and logistics by reducing costs, improving efficiency, and enhancing safety. As researchers, it is crucial to investigate the ethical and legal implications of using AI in transportation and logistics and ensure that AI systems are transparent and accountable.

AI for Marketing and Advertising: AI has the potential to transform marketing and advertising by providing personalized and targeted content, but it also raises concerns about privacy and manipulation. Researchers need to explore the implications of AI for marketing and advertising and investigate ways to ensure that AI systems are transparent and accountable.

AI for Agriculture and Farming: AI has the potential to optimize agriculture and farming by providing real-time monitoring, reducing waste, and enhancing crop yields. Researchers must investigate the ethical and legal implications of using AI in agriculture and farming and ensure that AI systems are transparent and accountable.

AI for Environmental Sustainability: AI has the potential to enhance environmental sustainability by monitoring and predicting environmental risks, optimizing resource use, and reducing waste. Researchers need to explore the implications of AI for environmental sustainability and investigate ways to ensure that AI systems are transparent and accountable.

AI for Entertainment and Media: AI has the potential to transform entertainment and media by personalizing content, enhancing user experience, and providing new forms of storytelling. As researchers, it is crucial to investigate the ethical and legal implications of using AI in entertainment and media and ensure that AI systems are transparent and accountable.

In conclusion, as academics and researchers, it is essential to explore the potential implications of AI in various sectors and investigate ways to ensure that AI systems are transparent and accountable. By doing so, we can harness the full potential of AI while minimizing its negative impacts.

THE ETHICAL
DILEMMA OF AI

THE ETHICS OF AI

Artificial intelligence has rapidly emerged as a transformative technology, revolutionizing various sectors and impacting society at large. However, the widespread adoption of AI systems also raises significant ethical concerns. This essay critically examines the ethical challenges associated with AI, including issues of privacy, fairness, accountability, and the potential for bias. By exploring these ethical dimensions, we aim to highlight the importance of responsible AI development and emphasize the need for ethical frameworks to guide its implementation.

The ethical implications of AI are multifaceted, requiring careful consideration as the technology continues to advance. As AI systems become more sophisticated and pervasive, it is imperative to address ethical challenges to ensure that AI development aligns with societal values, promotes fairness, and respects individual rights. This essay delves into the ethical issues surrounding AI, exploring privacy concerns, biases, accountability, and the need for responsible AI development.

AI systems often rely on vast amounts of personal data to train and operate effectively.

The collection, storage, and use of such data raise significant privacy concerns. Ethical considerations include obtaining informed consent, ensuring data security, and preventing unauthorized access. Striking a balance between data-driven innovation and protecting individual privacy is crucial to safeguarding fundamental human rights in the AI era.

AI systems are vulnerable to biases present in the data they are trained on, potentially perpetuating existing societal biases and discrimination. Ethical concerns arise when AI systems produce biased outcomes, such as in hiring processes or law enforcement. Addressing bias requires careful design, diverse and representative data sets, and ongoing monitoring to ensure fairness and prevent the exacerbation of societal inequalities.

As AI systems become more autonomous and make critical decisions, the issue of accountability becomes paramount. Determining responsibility for AI-generated actions, such as autonomous vehicles causing accidents or AI-powered financial systems making biased decisions, poses ethical challenges. Ensuring transparency in AI decision-making processes and establishing mechanisms for accountability are essential to address the ethical implications of AI technology.

The black-box nature of some AI algorithms raises ethical concerns regarding their decision-making processes. The lack of transparency and explainability hinders individuals' ability to understand, contest, or challenge AI-driven decisions that may significantly impact their lives. Ethical frameworks should emphasize the development of AI systems that are explainable and accountable, allowing individuals to trust and engage with AI technology.

The deployment of AI has the potential to reshape labor markets and contribute to employment disruptions. Ethical considerations arise concerning the impact of AI on job displacement, income inequality, and socio-economic disparities. Ensuring a just transition and considering the welfare of affected individuals is crucial in addressing the social implications of AI-driven automation.

The ethical challenges surrounding AI demand a proactive and responsible approach to its development and implementation. To foster a sustainable and beneficial AI ecosystem, it is essential to prioritize privacy protection, fairness, transparency, accountability, and the mitigation of biases. Collaborative efforts between stakeholders from academia, industry, and policymakers are necessary to establish robust ethical frameworks that guide AI development and ensure alignment with societal values. By addressing these ethical dimensions, society can harness the transformative potential of AI while upholding principles of fairness, equity, and human rights.

The main danger, however, will be the displacement of workers if AI replaces them. The rapid advancements in artificial intelligence (AI) have led to concerns about the potential displacement of human workers by AI systems. This essay critically examines the dangers associated with AI-driven automation, focusing on the displacement of workers and the potential consequences for employment and socio-economic well-being. By exploring the multifaceted dimensions of this issue, including technological advancements, economic implications, and ethical considerations, we aim to shed light on the challenges and propose strategies to mitigate the potential negative impacts.

The integration of AI-driven automation has the potential to transform industries and redefine the nature of work. However, this transformation also raises concerns about the displacement of human workers as AI systems increasingly perform tasks previously carried out by humans. This essay delves into the dangers associated with AI-driven automation, examining the potential consequences for workers, the economy, and society as a whole.

Technological Advancements and Labor Market Disruption

AI-driven automation has the potential to disrupt various sectors, including manufacturing, transportation, customer service, and data analysis. As AI systems become increasingly capable of performing complex tasks, there is a risk that certain job roles may become obsolete. The displacement of workers due to technological advancements can lead to unemployment, underemployment, and income inequality, posing significant challenges for individuals and society.

Economic Implications and Income Inequality

The displacement of workers by AI-driven automation can exacerbate existing income inequalities. Job losses and shifts in employment patterns may result in a concentration of wealth and power among those who control AI technologies. Economic disparities can widen, affecting both individuals and communities. The potential for increased income inequality raises ethical and social justice concerns, requiring proactive measures to address the adverse economic impacts of AI-driven automation.

Skills Mismatch and the Need for Reskilling

The displacement of workers by AI systems often stems from a mismatch between the skills demanded by the labor market and the skills possessed by workers. As AI automates routine tasks, the demand for cognitive and non-routine skills increases. Reskilling and upskilling programs become crucial to equip workers with the skills required in the evolving job market. Ensuring access to quality education and training programs can help mitigate the negative impacts of worker displacement and facilitate a smooth transition.

Ethical Considerations and the Future of Work

The ethical implications of AI-driven automation are of paramount importance. Society must grapple with questions of fairness, dignity, and the welfare of displaced workers. Ensuring a just transition and protecting the rights of workers become imperative. Ethical frameworks should guide the development and implementation of AI technologies, emphasizing the promotion of human well-being, the provision of social safety nets, and the equitable distribution of benefits.

Collaborative Solutions and Policy Interventions

Addressing the dangers of AI-driven displacement requires a collaborative approach involving policymakers, industry stakeholders, workers' organizations, and academia. Policy interventions may include creating supportive labor market policies, facilitating lifelong learning, fostering entrepreneurship, and promoting job creation in emerging sectors. Balancing innovation with social considerations is essential to navigate the complex landscape of AI-driven automation.

The displacement of workers by AI-driven automation poses significant dangers to the workforce, the economy, and society as a whole. However, by recognizing these dangers and implementing proactive strategies, the potential negative impacts can be mitigated. Ensuring a just transition, investing in reskilling programs, and upholding ethical principles are vital steps towards harnessing the benefits of AI while safeguarding the well-being of workers. By embracing collaborative and inclusive approaches, society can navigate the challenges and shape a future where AI-driven automation coexists harmoniously with human labor.

THE AI REVOLUTION

This section undertakes a comprehensive comparative analysis of two transformative eras in human history: the advent of artificial intelligence and the Industrial Revolution. By examining the similarities and differences between these two events, we seek to shed light on their profound impacts on society, economy, labor, and technological advancement. Through a multidimensional exploration, we explore the revolutionary nature, social implications, economic changes, and ethical considerations that accompany both the AI era and the Industrial Revolution.

The advent of AI and the Industrial Revolution have reshaped society and ushered in new waves of technological advancements. This article draws comparisons between these transformative epochs, exploring their similarities and differences to understand the broader implications for humanity.

Both AI and the Industrial Revolution brought about radical technological transformations. The Industrial Revolution introduced mechanical production methods, such as the steam engine and textile machinery, while AI represents a shift toward intelligent machines and automation. Both eras disrupted traditional modes of work, leading to significant changes in productivity and economic output.

The Industrial Revolution witnessed the mechanization of labor-intensive tasks, resulting in the displacement of workers and the rise of factory-based production. Similarly, AI-driven automation is poised to automate routine and repetitive tasks, potentially leading to job displacement in various sectors. However, the scope and nature of labor displacement differ, as AI has the potential to impact a broader range of occupations, including skilled professions.

AI and the Industrial Revolution have had profound economic effects. The Industrial Revolution ushered in a period of mass production, increased productivity, and the rise of capitalism. Similarly, AI has the potential to drive economic growth, enhance efficiency, and unlock new opportunities in various sectors. However, concerns exist regarding the concentration of wealth, income inequality, and the potential for job polarization.

Both AI and the Industrial Revolution have significant social implications. The Industrial Revolution led to urbanization, population shifts, and changes in living conditions. AI has the potential to reshape social interactions, disrupt traditional employment structures, and affect social cohesion. The social impacts of both eras highlight the need for robust policies and ethical frameworks to address the challenges arising from societal transformations.

Ethical considerations emerge in both the AI era and the Industrial Revolution. The Industrial Revolution raised concerns about worker rights, child labor, and exploitation. Similarly, the ethical dimensions of AI encompass issues such as privacy, data security, algorithmic bias, and the impact on human agency. The integration of AI necessitates ethical frameworks to guide responsible development, deployment, and use.

The advent of AI and the Industrial Revolution represent transformative epochs in human history. While there are parallels between these eras in terms of technological transformation, labor displacement, economic changes, and social implications, key differences exist. AI, with its capacity for intelligent decision-making and automation, brings unique challenges and opportunities. Recognizing the similarities and differences between these transformative events is vital for informed decision-making, ethical considerations, and shaping a future where AI and technology serve the betterment of humanity.